Scholars, Dollars, and Public Policy

The Authors

ERNEST W. LEFEVER is president of the Ethics and Public Policy Center. He received a B.D. and Ph.D. in Christian ethics from Yale University. He has been a foreign policy researcher at the Library of Congress, the Institute for Defense Analyses, the Brookings Institution, and the Johns Hopkins School of Advanced International Studies, and has taught at American, Maryland, and Georgetown universities. Among the books he has written or edited are *Ethics and United States Foreign Policy* (1957), *Profile of American Politics* (1960), *Arms and Arms Control* (1962), *Ethics and World Politics* (1972), *Nuclear Arms in the Third World: U.S. Policy Dilemma* (1979), and *Will Capitalism Survive?* (1979).

RAYMOND ENGLISH is vice president of the Ethics and Public Policy Center. He served in the British Army for six years and received first class honors in history at Trinity College, Cambridge University; he also did graduate work at Harvard University. From 1964 to 1979 he directed a social science textbook program, *Concepts and Inquiry,* at the Educational Research Council of America. He taught political science at Kenyon College for sixteen years and was also an instructor in the Department of Government at Harvard. In addition to textbooks he has written numerous articles on politics and education.

ROBERT L. SCHUETTINGER is a senior policy analyst in the White House Office of Policy Information. He received a B.A. in history from Queens College in New York and an M.A. from the University of Chicago, as well as a B. Phil. in political thought from St. Andrew's University in Scotland. He was the founding editor of *Policy Review.* Among the books he has written, edited, or co-authored are *The Conservative Tradition in European Thought* (1970), *Lord Acton: Historian of Liberty* (1977), *Forty Centuries of Wage and Price Controls* (1979), and *Tax-Based Incomes Policies: A Cure for Inflation* (1982). His contribution to this volume was made before he joined the White House staff.

Scholars, Dollars, and Public Policy

New Frontiers in Corporate Giving

Ernest W. Lefever,
Raymond English, and
Robert L. Schuettinger

Ethics and Public Policy Center
Washington, D.C.

THE ETHICS AND PUBLIC POLICY CENTER, established in 1976, conducts a program of research, writing, publications, and conferences to encourage debate on domestic and foreign policy issues among religious, educational, academic, business, political, and other leaders. A nonpartisan effort, the Center is supported by contributions (which are tax deductible) from foundations, corporations, and individuals. The authors alone are responsible for the views expressed in Center publications. The founding president of the Center is **Ernest W. Lefever.**

Library of Congress Cataloging in Publication Data
Lefever, Ernest W.
  Scholars, dollars, and public policy.
  Includes bibliographical references and index.
  1. Corporations—United States—Political activity.
2. Government consultants—United States. 3. Corporations—
United States—Charitable contributions. I. English, Raymond.
II. Schuettinger, Robert Lindsay, 1936-   III. Title.
JK467.L43   1983   322'.3'0973   82-25126
ISBN 0-89633-065-6 (pbk.)

$4.00

© **1983 by the Ethics and Public Policy Center.** All rights reserved.
Printed in the United States of America.

Contents

Foreword *by Robert F. Dee*   *vii*

1 Dollars, Scholars, and Public Policy   *1*
2 Corporate Giving and Public Policy   *13*
3 Policy Guidelines   *20*
4 Effectiveness Criteria   *30*
5 Reliable Sources of Information   *39*

   Appendix   *45*

   Notes   *57*

   Index of Names   *61*

Foreword

SCHOLARS, DOLLARS, AND PUBLIC POLICY is, among other things, a manual designed to help managers of corporations conduct an important kind of philanthropy the right way—in the interest of their stockholders. As such, it will be greeted with enthusiasm by the business community in America.

Effective corporate giving is not easy. It is almost as hard to achieve as sound public policy. But Dr. Lefever, Mr. English, and Dr. Schuettinger have helped point the way toward both. They have amplified and answered the challenge—first issued by Irving Kristol in 1977—for corporations to support associations of scholars, teachers, and intellectuals whose work contributes to the preservation of a strong private sector.

This book should encourage many more corporations to exert their proper influence on the formation of public policy. It will certainly help those that choose to.

To be credible and effective, public policy organizations and their scholars do not have to be completely disinterested. But they must be free and financially independent. For that reason, they need broad-based support—from a cross section of businesses and other private donors.

Supporting appropriate public policy groups, as we found at SmithKline (now SmithKline Beckman Corporation) in the late 1970s, is well worthwhile. The Corporation had the eventual satisfaction of seeing some good ideas from those groups put into practice in the 1980s. We also received valuable scholarly support for our own participation in discussions of public policy. By combining informed independent commentary with common-sense advertising technique, for example, we helped alert millions of citizens to issues crucial to their well-being. In the process we gained many new friends and supporters.

In my view, business should play as direct and active a part as possible in the discussion of policy issues. But for many corporations, indirect participation in public debate may be preferable. To managers of all companies, then, I recommend this highly useful volume. By producing it, Dr. Lefever and his colleagues at the Ethics and Public Policy Center have greatly aided the cause of good government in a free society.

ROBERT F. DEE, *Chairman*
SmithKline Beckman Corporation

November 1982

CHAPTER ONE

Dollars, Scholars, and Public Policy

Corporate giving remains the last major underdeveloped frontier for private giving to philanthropic causes.
FILER COMMISSION, 1976

ON JANUARY 11, 1977, Henry Ford II startled the corporate and academic worlds by abruptly resigning from the board of the Ford Foundation, established and funded by his grandfather in 1936. The story made the front page of the *New York Times*. Mr. Ford had served on the board since 1943, as its chairman 1950-56. But in a bluntly worded letter to his board colleagues, he wrote that he could no longer in good conscience participate in or support an organization that in his view was undermining the very system that made the American economic miracle possible and thus benefited all citizens.

The Ford Foundation is the richest and most influential organization of its kind in the world. By that time it had disbursed over $4 billion for numerous projects in the United States and abroad, all intended to improve the lot of mankind by encouraging freedom, justice, and economic well-being. But some of these projects, in Ford's view, had had the opposite effect. Some Ford-financed institutions and scholars denounced "competitive enterprise" though they were quite content to live off "the fruits of our economic system," he said.

A significant portion of the abundance created by U.S. business enables the Foundation and like institutions to carry on their work. In effect, the Foundation is a creature of capitalism—a statement that I'm sure would be shocking to many professional staff people in the field of philanthropy. It is hard to discern recognition of this fact in anything the Foundation does. It is even more difficult to find an understanding of this in many of our institutions, particularly the universities, that are the beneficiaries of the Foundation's grant programs.[1]

Ford concluded with an ironic understatement: "The system that makes the Foundation possible very probably is worth preserving."

Ford's comments echoed what other perceptive observers had said earlier and anticipated a rising tide of criticism from academics, politicians, and corporate executives. His candor and courage gave momentum to the growing determination of corporate America not to feed the mouth that was biting it. Mr. Ford had issued a sturdy call for a more responsible philanthropy in the public policy arena.

Business Corporations and Public Policy

This study will deal with one facet, perhaps the most important facet, of corporate philanthropy—contributions by American business designed to influence a wide range of domestic and foreign policies. But first we must develop a working definition of the business corporation. Then we need to see how corporations, both by inadvertence and by design, affect the answers to specific political, economic, and social questions and the general direction of public policy itself.

The business corporation is a powerful, vital, and highly influential institution in American society. Its character and significance have been distorted by critics and uncritical admirers alike. Historians have neglected it. The press and the public have often misunderstood it. In 1979, Frances FitzGerald found that no contemporary high school textbook has "even the most general description of the modern corporation." "There is a near-ban on the terms 'conglomerate' and 'multinational corporation,'" she said; "the word 'corporation' tends to come up only in the context of the environmental movement—which is surely to put the cart before the horse."[2] In contrast, she quoted a widely used textbook written by Charles and Mary Beard in 1923. The Beards characterized the corporation as the "striking feature of American business life, one of the most marvelous institutions of all time, comparable in wealth and power and the number of its servants with kingdoms and states of old."[3]

The business corporation is an organization of persons that is chartered by the state to perform specific functions, occasionally cultural, sometimes political, but usually economic—the production and distribution of goods and services. Since the days of medieval Europe, corporations have been sanctioned by law and government. As the German political theorist Otto von Gierke pointed out, they became centers of resistance to monopolistic state authority—or, in John Kenneth Galbraith's phrase, centers of "countervailing power." In his famous *Dartmouth College* decision in 1819, Chief Justice John Marshall stressed the "immortality" of the corporation, which permits it to act "as a single individual" over time, "to manage its own affairs and to hold property without perplexing intricacies. . . . It is chiefly for the purpose of clothing bodies of men in succession with these qualities and capacities that corporations were invented."[4]

For our purposes, a business corporation is an economic institution chartered (but not created) by the state for specific purposes, regulated by corporate law, capitalized by the sale of stocks and bonds to the public, governed by a board of directors, and managed by executives. Unless it fails to make a profit or is swept aside by catastrophe it is endowed with immortality—it survives from one generation to the next. With this legitimacy and the capacity to act as a hog butcher, a player with railroads, an oil producer, or a computer manufacturer, the modern corporation has had an immense though unquantifiable impact on society. But it has been only one of the primary forces that mold the character and destiny of the American people. It competes for influence with the family, the church, the academy, the arts, science and technology, law, and the state itself, as well as with the forces of nature.

Here we are concerned primarily with the corporation's multiple impact on *public policy*, that is, on the broad public decisions that affect the distribution of power and resources in an organized society. "Public policy" is a delightfully ambiguous term—hence its utility. To describe it broadly and formally, public policy reflects the totality of decisions—supported by the power to give them effect—emerging from the interplay of forces and interests in the modern state. The major mechanisms that channel, moderate, and sometimes lead the incessant struggle for power, purpose, and influence are the government and the economic market. So defined, public policy can be seen as a drama whose principal actors are the government (executive, legislative, and judicial branches), the market, the corporation, trade unions, and a host of other organized interests. Ultimately the decisions are made by citizen-consumers by their votes at the ballot box and in the marketplace.

We will use the term *public policy* more narrowly, to refer only to decisions and actions in which the government is a major actor. Public policy includes foreign policy, monetary policy, fiscal policy, national security policy, and policy on more specific matters, such as energy, housing, health, the environment, public safety, crime, civil rights, education, inflation, unemployment, and agriculture.

Public policy deals with the public agenda writ large—issues that affect everyone in society. This means the government must either be actively involved by having a mandate for direct responsibility or be explicitly excluded from acting. The U.S. airline industry provides a good example: Should the government run the airlines, regulate them heavily, regulate them only in the areas of safety, or not regulate them at all? These questions add up to a major public issue. After the basic policy question is answered, a host of specific questions must be addressed.

In pluralistic America with its separation of powers and its multiplicity of pressure and interest groups, public policy decisions emerge from a process that is less than tidy or fully rational. But most Americans believe that the system has worked reasonably well. Every citizen or organized group has many opportunities to influence public decisions by supporting a political party or candidate, by lobbying, by using the communications media, and by exercising the fundamental rights of freedom of speech and assembly.

How Corporations Influence Public Issues

Business corporations, especially the larger ones, have a multiple impact on public policy. Their influence falls into six general categories. The first two listed below are largely non-deliberate, while the other four entail deliberate attempts by corporate leaders to influence general policy or to shape particular decisions. Corporations affect public policy:

1. *By their normal operations.*

A business corporation through its day-by-day operations—manufacturing, distributing, and selling goods, meeting a payroll, selling stock, borrowing money, paying taxes, distributing dividends—is an important actor in the economy and society generally and thus affects a variety of government policies. The structural complexities of the oil industry, for instance, have had a major effect on government policies of the past decade.

2. *By product and service advertising.*

Virtually all corporations advertise in the public media. For the most part public advertising presents the case for purchasing that corporation's product rather than a competitor's, but in the case of monopolies (such as local power companies) or near-monopolies (such as AT&T), the purpose is to foster good will toward the corporation. Both kinds of messages have multiple consequences, some of which impinge upon the public policy arena. For instance, advertising has an effect on the survival and character of newspapers and journals as well as of commercial radio and TV.

3. *By issue advertising.*

Since the early 1970s a new form of what used to be called institutional advertising has arisen. This advertising goes well beyond attempts to create institutional good will. It addresses larger public issues, often bearing some relation to the sponsoring corporation. For example, the Mobil Corporation, a leader in issue advertising, frequently deals with questions related to the petroleum industry, OPEC, and government regulations, though it addresses many other public issues as well.[5] In 1981, Mobil in ads supported the Reagan administration's moves to deregulate oil and criticized what it considered an unfair and distorted image of businessmen on TV programs. Other corporations active in issue advertising are SmithKline Beckman (formerly SmithKline), United Technologies, and Chase Manhattan Bank. Obviously, advertising addressed to such questions as government regulation, entitlement programs, and capital formation has, or at least is designed to have, a more direct impact on public debate than normal business advertising.

4. *By lobbying.*

The right of individuals or interest groups to "lobby" Congress or the executive branch is explicit in the First Amendment, which specifies the right "to petition the government for a redress of grievances." Economic interests, whether railroads, bankers, or farmers, have not hesitated to exercise this right. Because of their omnipresence in Washington, their numbers (15,000),[6] and their influence, lobbyists of all persuasions have collectively been called the "Fourth Branch of Government." James Madison in the *Federalist Papers* spoke of "factions," and expressed the hope that one strong special interest would tend to balance off another and that the resulting decisions of the federal government would serve the common good. Obviously this has not always happened. Many regulations and much subsidy legislation are the direct result of lobbying by major business associations such as the National Association of Manufacturers and the Chamber of Commerce, by particular industries and trade unions, and by farm, consumer, environmental, and other groups.

5. *By direct political activity.*

A relatively recent development has been the direct involvement of corporations in the campaigns of local, state, and national candidates for political office. Since the passage of the Federal Election Reform Act of 1974, when corporations were given the same legal right as trade unions to form political action committees, business leaders have been active in supporting candidates who were expected to pursue policies they favored. According to the Federal Election Commission, Political Action Committees (PACs) spent more than $131 million in the 1979-80 federal elections.[7] This total was divided among six categories of PACs: Corporation, Labor Organizations, Non-Connected (not connected to any organization), "Trade/Member/Health," Cooperative, and "Corporation without Stock." Of these, Corporation PACs disbursed $31.4 million, and Labor PACs $25 million. Neither Corporation nor Labor PACs outspent the third and fourth categories, whose outlays were: Non-Connected, $38.5 million, and "Trade/Member/Health," $32 million.

Because of the importance of energy, the problems posed by OPEC, and the plethora of U.S. government regulations, American oil companies have been particularly active politically. According to David Rogers, "Federal Election Commission records show that oil contributions rose by at least $2.38 million in the last [1980] election, a 111 per cent increase that was more than four times the rate of growth in general campaign spending.... Oil contributions to Republicans grew more than twice the rate of those to Democrats."[8]

Yet the direct support of political candidates by businesses is usually not an ideological or partisan enterprise. It is more like purchasing insurance through investment in legislators who exercise considerable influence or in candidates who have a good chance of winning. It is a matter of prudence to have friends at court, irrespective of their party affiliation. However, the oil companies' 1980 record suggests that corporate intervention in elections may become more openly "political." Two years before that the Supreme Court had upheld the right of a corporation to engage in direct defense of a position favorable to its own interest in a political referendum campaign (*First National Bank* [of Boston] v. *Bellotti*).[9]

Invoking Madison's hope of a vigorous encounter among "factions," one can only applaud the recent involvement of business in direct political action to counterbalance trade unions and special anti-business, anti-market groups that have long lobbied directly and participated actively in political campaigns.

6. *By contributions to public policy groups.*

Traditional corporate philanthropy tends to focus on the communities where the corporate headquarters or branch offices are located and includes relatively non-controversial charities such as the United Way, hospitals, Boy Scouts, community enterprises, and the arts. Its purpose is to enrich society and to generate good will for the corporation. Traditional giving also includes contributions to specific university chairs, departments, or students in the fields of the corporation's interest. Exxon, for example, announced in September 1981 a $15 million program to help ease the shortage of engineering professors by supporting doctoral students planning to teach engineering and providing salary supplements for untenured engineering professors.[10]

In contrast, public policy giving is designed primarily to influence the debate over, and ultimately the outcome of, controversial issues. Corporations can engage in this debate directly through political action, or less directly by supporting selected public policy causes and organizations, of which there are literally hundreds. Some of these groups, such as those associated with Ralph Nader's consumer movement, are action-oriented. Others, like the Brookings Institution, are more academically inclined. Their size, competence, style, and constituency vary greatly, but they can be said to fall into a dozen or so substantive or issue categories. The Foundation for Public Affairs lists a hundred such groups under eleven working areas in the 1982 edition of its *Public Interest Profiles*.[11] The areas are listed below with examples.

1. Civil / Human Rights
    Amnesty International, New York
    Women's Equity Action League, Washington
2. Community / Grassroots
    Center for Community Change, Washington
    Citizen's Choice, Washington
3. Consumer / Health
    Center for Auto Safety, Washington
    Consumer Alert, Modesto, California
4. Corporate / Governmental Accountability
    Common Cause, Washington
    National Taxpayers Union, Washington
5. Economic System
    Law and Economics Center, Atlanta, Georgia
    Public Interest Economics Center, Washington
6. Energy / Environment
    Americans for Energy Independence, Washington
    The Wilderness Society, Washington

7. Foreign Policy / Defense
    American Security Council, Boston, Virginia
    Center for Defense Information, Washington
8. Media
    Accuracy in Media, Washington
    National News Council, New York
9. Political Process / Political Action
    Conservative Caucus, Vienna, Virginia
    National Committee for an Effective Congress, New York
10. Public Interest Law
    Center for Law and Social Policy, Washington
    Pacific Legal Foundation, Sacramento, California
11. Public Policy Research
    American Enterprise Institute, Washington
    Brookings Institution, Washington
    Ethics and Public Policy Center, Washington
    Institute for Policy Studies, Washington

The list illustrates the range of interests and political orientation of the public policy organizations currently supported by private or government grants (though some of those listed do not receive funds from corporations). They span the spectrum from left to right, representing views from pro to con on such basic matters as the market, limited government, and a strong defense.

Any corporate board, chief executive officer, or contributions committee interested in supporting public policy groups has a veritable supermarket to choose from. This study seeks to clarify the options available and to suggest guidelines to help corporate leaders make responsible contributions decisions that serve their policy preferences. Though these preferences may differ from corporation to corporation, one may safely assume that the views of American business leadership fall well within the broad policy consensus of our remarkably united yet pluralistic society.

Growing Criticism of Corporate Philanthropy

Since the mid-1950s a growing number of critics have attacked what they regard as foolish, self-defeating, and even dangerous philanthropy by both large and small corporations and businessmen. Among them are a leading industrialist, David Packard; a former secretary of the treasury, William E. Simon; a social philosopher, Irving Kristol; an economist, C. Lowell Harriss; a university president, W. Allen Wallis; and a political philosopher, Michael Novak.

In October 1973, David Packard, since 1958 a member of the Committee for Corporate Support of American Universities, told a gathering of Stanford alumni that despite his strong devotion to the cause of the private university and his belief that universities play a vital role in American life, he could no longer endorse unrestricted giving to them.[12] Instead, he insisted that corporations should ask, quite simply, "What, if anything, do we get in return for our money?" "Hostile groups of scholars," Packard said, "are, to a large degree, responsible for the anti-business bias of many of our young people today. And I do not believe it is in the corporate interest to support them. . . ." Corporate leaders have a responsibility to their stockholders "to be sure the money contributed will, in some defensible way," benefit them and the corporation, he said. "In the future, let's focus our money and our energy on those schools and departments which are strong and which also contribute in some specific way to our individual companies, or to the general welfare of our free enterprise system."

In March 1976, then Secretary of the Treasury William E. Simon discussed corporate giving to academic institutions in a letter to the president of the American Council on Education.[13] "I do not suggest," Simon wrote, "that gift giving be conditioned on the institutions' presenting only the views I believe in. But should they be supported if they present only the views I do not believe in, especially when I perceive such views to be a direct threat to our economic and personal freedoms? . . . Teachers are given a rare privilege in having access to the instruction of students. They should not violate that trust by concentrating on only one approach or by consciously attempting to bias their students. Diversity of opinion and dissent are both necessary and desirable for a democratic system such as ours to function properly."

Irving Kristol in 1977 observed in an influential essay that "the majority of foundations in this country, like most of our major universities, exude a climate of opinion wherein an anti-business bent becomes a perfectly natural inclination."[14] But we should not, he said, "exaggerate or be dogmatic about this situation. Those foundations and universities are not homogeneous or totalitarian institutions; not all divisions and departments have identical attitudes; nor are these attitudes themselves consistently sovereign."

Also in 1977, Columbia University economist C. Lowell Harriss, noting the crucial role corporations play in our democratic society and the strength of their critics, asked: "Why do corporations contribute relatively little (less than one-tenth of 1 per cent of profits) to public policy activities?"[15] He suggested two main reasons: First, corporations are, with justification, skeptical about the results of many public policy programs. They perceive the management of some non-profit organizations to be of poor quality. Second, corporations are rightly concerned that if they donate to a worthy-sounding cause (such as the conservation of the environment, or consumer protection, or even peace movements) they may, in the end, be aiding their adversaries. Harriss noted that it is difficult and costly to discover effective friends and to direct resources to them, and that not every corporation is able or willing to do this.

At about this time, W. Allen Wallis, then president of the University of Rochester (now U.S. under secretary of state for economic affairs), who as a professor of economics has been a staunch defender of academic freedom, wrote:

> People who believe in a free society, in limited government, in individualism, in private property, in free enterprise, and in a market economy are, with a few notable exceptions, remarkably indiscriminate in their support of intellectual activities, including universities, research organizations, and public information programs. They are at least as likely to support activities that are part of the problem as to support those that can do something about it. To some extent this is because they do not understand how public opinion is formed. To some extent it is because they are interested only in quick results—meaning before the next election—when they should think in terms of generations. To some extent they simply lack the sophistication to know which of the counter currents have the qualities that will make an impact on honest intellectuals.[16]

Wallis then quoted Milton Friedman: "If businessmen are truly concerned about the threat to our free economy, they can do something about it by devoting the same care to their gifts as to their purchases."

Writing in 1978, Michael Novak urged the business community to play an active role in the "war of ideas," which is largely "carried on *outside* the university, or in the part of a professor's life conducted in public, outside the classroom"—in "journals and magazines, in papers and books, in lectures and debates, on 'talk shows' and newscasts."[17] Novak went on to urge corporations to pursue a positive political education program, "a political strategy that step-by-step meets that of the new class." (The "new class" consists of intellectuals, usually of the left, and their allies in the media elite. Often corporations unwittingly subsidize "new class" ideas by supporting universities and other organizations.[18]) To counter the tactics of the new class, Novak recommended:

> Modern corporations need to recognize the new element of ideological warfare in their own business environment. They need to enlist university study groups and independent intellectual organizations of several sorts: (1) to set forth their own vision of the world, with its intellectual and moral underpinnings, and its own connections to what they are actually doing; and (2) to rebut the opposing ideologies and accusations launched by the new class.[19]

In the following chapters, we will suggest how corporations can play a significant role in this war of ideas. First we will sketch a brief history of corporate philanthropy in this country, and the development of public policy giving. Next we will suggest policy guidelines to help corporations determine which public policy groups share their political philosophy and what the relation between donor and recipient should be. Then we will develop criteria for judging which groups are performing most effectively. We will conclude by citing reliable sources of information on public policy organizations.

CHAPTER TWO

Corporate Giving and Public Policy

LONG AFTER LARGE AMERICAN business corporations came into being in the early nineteenth century, philanthropy continued to be an individual, not a corporate, activity. The great American entrepreneurs made their grants and bequests from their personal wealth, not on behalf of their businesses. Indeed, their economic philosophy precluded the mixing of business and benevolence. So did the laws governing corporations.

In the late nineteenth century, public-spirited "robber barons" made numerous personal grants to the arts, hospitals, and educational institutions. Between 1873 and 1911, entrepreneur Johns Hopkins established the Johns Hopkins University and Hospital; John D. Rockefeller, the University of Chicago; Chauncey Depew, Drexel Institute; Philip Danforth Armour, the Armour Institute of Technology; and Leland Stanford, Stanford University. Robert S. Brookings, after establishing the Washington University Medical School in St. Louis, went on to found the Brookings Institution in Washington, D.C., in 1928, "to collect, interpret, and lay before the country in clear and intelligent form the fundamental economic facts concerning which opinions need to be formed"; this became the first privately operated public policy research and publication organization in the United States, and possibly in the world. Andrew Carnegie endowed several organizations: the Carnegie Foundation for the Advancement of Teaching, the Carnegie Institution (for research), the Carnegie Foundation (for science and the humanities), the Carnegie Endowment for International Peace, and the Church Peace Union (now called the Council on Religion and International Affairs).[1]

This list of personal philanthropy could easily be lengthened. Occasionally economic pragmatists, such as Justice Oliver Wendell Holmes, worried about these vast withdrawals of potential investment capital from the market. Personal philanthropy continues in our day, finding its most lavish expression in the Rockefeller and Ford foundations.

Beginnings of Corporate Philanthropy

During the early boom of business incorporations, *circa* 1820-70, state laws restricted corporations rigidly to functions specified in their charters. They were not allowed to use profits—which were viewed as the property of the shareholders—for altruistic purposes. Most court decisions maintained that a corporation had to demonstrate a direct economic benefit to its shareholders to justify any kind of charitable donation of corporate funds. The railroads in the late nineteenth century, for instance, were able to pay large parts of the costs of erecting YMCA hostels in many small cities, on the grounds that the YMCAs provided inexpensive lodging for railroad employees.

When corporations began to engage in philanthropy, they rarely contributed large endowment funds. They were constrained from doing this by their desire to respect the wishes of their shareholders. They usually made short-term grants of one to five years, renewable only if the donor was satisfied with the way the money was used.

The first major example in the United States of corporate philanthropy not directly related to business requirements was support for the wartime Red Cross drive in 1917. Even then, corporations made their donations indirectly by declaring a special Red Cross dividend and sending it to their stockholders with a letter urging them to donate the money to the Red Cross war fund. At least 148 corporations did this, and the stockholders who responded raised

$17 million for the Red Cross. This experience helped prompt the gradual broadening of the laws on corporate gifts.[2]

In 1936, the Internal Revenue Act was amended to permit corporations to take tax deductions of up to 5 per cent of their net income for contributions to educational or other charitable purposes. Marion R. Fremont-Smith notes in his book *Philanthropy and the Business Corporation* (1972) that "with a current tax rate of 22 per cent on the first $25,000 of corporate income and of 48 per cent on income in excess of that amount, the deduction for corporate charitable gifts can be translated into a 'cost' that is not insubstantial. For example, a corporation with income of $100,000 saves $480 in taxes for each $1,000 in contributions: its 'cost' for the corporation is $520."[3]

Corporate giving as a percentage of net income has hovered around 1 per cent since 1945, despite the allowable tax deduction of up to 5 per cent of net profits. As a result of the Economic Recovery Act of 1981, corporations may now claim a tax deduction for donations of up to 10 per cent. This means that corporations could make tax-deductible contributions of approximately $25 billion in 1982.

The requirement that a corporation must demonstrate a "direct benefit" to itself (that is, to its shareholders) before it can make a charitable donation was to all intents and purposes repealed in 1953, when the New Jersey Supreme Court decided the case of *A. P. Smith Manufacturing Company* v. *Barlow*. The court upheld a gift of $1,000 to Princeton University, stating that "in our view the corporate power to make reasonable charitable contributions exists under modern conditions."[4] By 1971, forty-eight states had enacted legislation specifically allowing corporations to make reasonable charitable gifts from stockholder funds.

Corporate giving results from a variety of motives, of which W. Allen Wallis has made this useful five-fold classification: (1) *defensive public relations* or *appeasement* designed to deflect harassment, hostile publicity, or boycotts; (2) *positive public relations* to keep workers happy and to contribute to public good will; (3) *focused benefits* to the company, such as educational grants for workers and their families and support of research useful to the corporation; (4) *general benefits* to the company, such as grants to improve the communities where plants are located; and (5) *indirect, long-term, and unpredictable benefits* to the company. This last category covers grants to basic research, national cultural institutions, and medical schools; Wallis includes here public policy research that favors the maintenance of freedom—legal, political, and economic.[5]

The Social Responsibility of Business

Although the courts have decided that corporate officials have the legal right to spend some of their stockholders' money for charitable purposes and the U.S. Congress has confirmed and even encouraged this right by granting a tax deduction for these donations, the underlying philosophical and ethical issues have not been resolved. Many people who have thought about the relationships among business, society, and the government conclude that the idea of the "social responsibility of business" is confusing, misleading, or even without merit.

Extreme opponents of corporate philanthropy, such as economist Milton Friedman, argue that the sole business of business is business—that is, to make a profit, and as large a profit as possible. In this view, a healthy profit guarantees that the business is contributing to the public good by providing needed goods or services; therefore, profitable corporations automatically discharge their duty to society, as long as they obey the law. Friedman concludes that if businessmen wish to help worthy causes, they should do so as individuals, using their own and not the stockholders' funds.

He does, however, suggest two loopholes, which as Lee Smith observed "bring his philosophy pretty much into line with corporate charity as actually practiced."[6] The first is that corporations owned by their managers may give to charity in order to cut taxes; the second is that gifts to institutions serving workers in a plant (local hospital, college, museum, park) are justified, since these institutions help the company attract and retain good workers.

In practice, Friedman has accepted corporate support for his own educational efforts, such as funding for his successful Public Broadcasting Service TV program "Free to Choose," aired in 1980. He has also accepted corporate grants for distributing information about his proposal for an educational voucher program. These two practical exceptions lend support to the principle of corporate giving to public policy institutions whose work promotes a free society and its market economy, causes that Professor Friedman champions.

Some businessmen, however, persist in the view that it is wrong for a corporation to engage in philanthropy at the shareholders' expense. They argue that even a gift to a hospital that serves corporation workers or to a college that provides technicians and managers is unjustifiable. One corporation recently invited each shareholder to indicate precisely how his or her share of the corporation's tax-exempt charitable fund should be used.[7] Other executives argue that the *only* justifiable corporate giving is support of political causes that can enhance the corporation's capacity to make profits now and in the future. (This would include sympathetic public policy organizations.) However, they would prefer to give this money *before* declaring profits, that is, to regard them as a business expense and to forgo the charitable tax exemption offered by Congress (though the net tax advantage would be the same either way).

In striking contrast to these principles of restraint is the notion that business has broad social responsibilities and, beyond that, that each corporation should be subject to a "social audit." The social audit idea calls for an evaluation of a corporation's behavior according to a checklist of social goals, such as full employment, health, clean air, and safety. The performance of a particular business can thus be portrayed on a balance sheet similar to a financial audit, in which a firm's "debits" to society would be assessed against its "credits." A ton of air pollution may, for example, be traded off against a grant for a new operating room in the local hospital. The approach has a number of flaws, not the least of which is the difficulty of quantifying the corporation's positive and negative effects on society.

The social audit idea came to prominence in the 1970s, during the heyday of the environmental movement. It was fostered in part by the general climate of hostility toward corporations and especially toward multinational firms. Corporate executives often found it safer to pay "protection money" in the form of social audit gestures rather than to struggle against the pressure groups and protesters. Those were the days when a tiny fish called the snail darter was exploited effectively to close down a vast hydroelectric project, and when nuclear power stations remained half-built while millions of dollars were spent on litigation as construction costs soared far beyond original estimates.

The Aetna Life and Casualty Company of Connecticut has taken social factors into account in a novel way. It estimates that the total cost to society from arson (including lost tax revenues, rebuilding expenses, funding for police and fire departments) comes close to $8 billion a year. As an insurance company, Aetna has an interest in reducing arson, an interest shared by society as a whole. Hence, Aetna has embarked on an anti-arson campaign by making a grant of $95,000 to the city of New Haven, Connecticut, to develop an early-warning system that will alert police and fire departments to the areas of the city where arson is most likely to occur. Aetna has also contributed to the costs of conducting seminars for authorities in various cities to improve their techniques of investigating arson.[8]

Support for Public Policy Purposes

Public policy giving includes support for organizations, movements, and individuals seeking to influence a wide range of government policies, domestic and foreign, mainly by producing and disseminating studies, ideas, facts, and recommendations for academic, business, public policy, and other leaders. Tax-exempt organizations, by law, are severely limited in their right to lobby for or against specific legislative proposals;[9] they concentrate instead on what may be broadly called public affairs education, which helps create the intellectual and conceptual environment in which public policy decisions—in political parties, legislative bodies, the executive departments, and even the courts—are made. As we have noted, corporations also spend considerable funds on *direct* political activities, both lobbying and supporting candidates in elections; however, our concern here is with corporate giving to tax-exempt public policy causes that bear less immediately, though no less significantly, on the quality of public life in America.

According to a 1980 Conference Board survey, approximately 5 per cent of all corporate giving is devoted to "public policy purposes." That 5 per cent was divided this way in 1978: 1.7 per cent to economic education, 1.6 to environmental and ecological causes, .05 to legal concerns, and 1.1 to non-university research organizations.[10] If the sample of 759 companies in the survey is roughly representative of corporate giving in general, then of the total donations "for public policy purposes," public policy *institutions* probably receive a good deal less than half. In 1980, the public policy 5 per cent of corporate giving amounted to approximately $125 million. Public policy institutions, then, probably received much less than $62 million that year.

Since the early 1970s there has been a definite trend toward increased public policy giving, but how much and to what groups remain lively issues. The underlying premise of this study is that the objectives of business and of a free society will both be served by active corporate participation in the decisions that affect the quality of American life, and that one effective way for business to be responsibly involved is to support appropriate public policy causes and organizations. The following two chapters develop policy and effectiveness guidelines for evaluating public policy groups.

CHAPTER THREE

Policy Guidelines

MOST CORPORATION EXECUTIVES regard corporate giving not as charity but as an investment from which they expect short-term or long-term returns. They agree that contributions should be a "cool and reasoned investment in the future of the firm" rather than a "form of institutional kindness."[1] But though many large firms now include in their philanthropic budgets a formal or informal public policy category, few have a developed philosophy for determining which organizations to support.

In 1976, a Business Advisory Committee to the Commission on Private Philanthropy and Public Needs recommended that the contributions and other public service activities of corporations "receive the same quality of management attention that other corporate functions receive and deserve with carefully thought-out policies and goals characteristic of well-managed activities."[2] The essential elements in a well-managed program, said the committee, include "clearly defined policies and goals; budgeting for contributions and public service activities; well organized screening and administrative procedures; application of performance standards to new and ongoing grants."

Corporate donations are generally determined and given either directly, by a *contributions committee* that includes major executives (or by a public affairs office), or less directly, through a *company foundation*. Some corporations contribute to public policy causes by both means simultaneously—grants from contributions committees or public affairs budgets and foundation grants; examples are Exxon and Mobil.

The *committee* approach varies from an informal and sometimes haphazard arrangement to a carefully structured plan with a professional contributions staff.

Corporate *foundations* receive all their funds from the parent firm, usually in the form of working capital donated annually. (In contrast, independent foundations usually have a permanent endowment.) Boards of corporate foundations generally include outside specialists, such as hospital directors and university presidents, as well as representatives from top management. An advantage to the foundation method of making contributions is that if the foundation builds up reserves in prosperous years, it can maintain grants when company profits drop.

In 1980, a Conference Board survey of 732 companies showed that about half had a foundation. Among the large companies that do are United States Steel, Alcoa, and General Motors.

In deciding whether to support a particular public policy organization, corporate officials should apply two partially overlapping sets of criteria. First, *policy:* What are the organization's political principles and approach? Second, *effectiveness:* Does the organization have a reputation for accomplishing its objectives? (Or, if it is new, do the persons in charge inspire confidence?) How long is it likely to survive? Is it financially sound? (Or, if new, does it justify a "risk" investment?)

The two sets of considerations are equally important, but policy questions should be addressed first. If the philosophy and goals of the potential recipient are unacceptable to the donor, the matter can be closed at that point, without the need to examine the more elusive questions of effectiveness. In this chapter we will look at policy criteria, and in the next, effectiveness criteria.

Examining Philosophy and Goals

The importance of policy criteria is so self-evident that it is often disregarded. As Irving Kristol said after Henry Ford II resigned from the Ford Foundation board: "The sad truth is that the business community has never thought seriously about its philanthropy, and doesn't know how."[3] Kristol went on to define donations intended to support public policy institutions as *controllable* expenditures. That is, they are donations about which corporations should be much more critically selective than they need be about *mandated* expenditures, such as support for local hospitals and the United Way.

There is much truth in the maxim attributed to Henry Ford I, "Never give anything without strings attached,"[4] though Ford was apparently unable to follow this precept in endowing the Ford Foundation. While corporations cannot retract contributions to groups whose efforts subsequently arouse misgivings, they can make the recipients aware of their concern. It is prudent also, especially with unproven recipients, to make short-term grants with the possibility of renewal, rather than long-term grants.

Public policy causes and organizations are necessarily controversial. A corporate director or a shareholder may object to a grant for a particular policy institute because he disagrees with its philosophy or he regards it as "too risky." Hence, some corporations do not contribute to policy groups. Others hedge their bets by simultaneously supporting organizations with opposing views; one outspoken corporate official has complained that too many chief executive officers "want to be all things to all men." An expert in corporate philanthropy has denounced the tendency of some corporate executives to appease "the counterculture." Thus, for example, dozens of firms have supported Ralph Nader's activities, which many observers believe are more anti-business than pro-consumer.[5]

The words and ideas generated by public policy groups do make a difference, and so a deliberate policy of giving or withholding support on a policy basis will have consequences both for business and for American society. The decision to support either an extreme environmentalist group or one that takes seriously the need for productivity, a strident single-cause group or a more general and moderate research group, has consequences. And a thoughtful calculation of the probable effects, both short- and long-term, is essential for responsible giving.

In judging the positions of policy centers, corporate executives should use their own values as a measuring rod. One basic principle is that they should not support projects inimical to a free society in which corporations can flourish and *should* support those that seek to preserve a dynamic private sector. If they believe in limited government and freedom of choice, including freedom of enterprise, they should not, for instance, give general grants to universities in which a substantial number of professors are hostile to these values. (According to a 1981 survey, 74 per cent of American Political Science Association members—most of whom are college teachers—classify themselves as "moderately liberal" or "very liberal," while only 15 per cent call themselves "conservative." The same poll showed 61 per cent Democrats and 10 per cent Republicans.[6] In America, to be "liberal" is to favor substantial government control of the economy and substantial government intervention in the life of the family, school, and culture generally.)

The following six questions can help donors ascertain where a potential recipient stands on crucial points:

1. What is the proper role of government in relation to other institutions in society (the family, the church, the economic market, educational institutions, labor unions, voluntary associations)?

2. Are political and religious freedom possible without a free market and freedom of expression?

3. What are the chief threats to U.S. security from abroad?

4. What are the most serious political (or social or economic) problems facing the United States?

5. Does the United States need more or less central planning? More or less regulation of business?

6. What should the U.S. policy approach be in the following areas:
    a. Energy conservation and development
    b. Environmental concerns vs. productivity
    c. Development in the Third World
    d. The superpower balance or imbalance
    e. Improvement of educational institutions
    f. Equal opportunity for minorities and women

Answers to major questions like these must be largely gleaned from an organization's publications and from informal conversations with its officers, not through a formal interview or questionnaire. Help is available from several reliable sources of information (see chapter five).

A Multiple-Consideration Ethic

All public issues are complex and many-faceted, no matter how desirable the goal and how simple the proposed means appear to be. Everyone wants clean air *and* fuel-efficient cars. Everyone cares about preserving landscapes and forests, but everyone also wants affordable fuel and wood. Everyone would like lower defense costs, but most Americans want the United States to be strong enough to deter Soviet aggression and withstand nuclear blackmail. Public issues, like our great social objectives—freedom, justice, security, order, and productivity—are intertwined. The utopians, great simplifiers, and single-issue advocates fail to see the larger picture. Regrettably, they often dominate public policy causes and organizations.

Realism, an ability to distinguish what can from what cannot be done, is the beginning of political wisdom. Politics is the art of the possible, and prudent compromise is always necessary. The man who says "a plague on both your houses" is a utopian cynic. The man who insists that the strongest force must prevail, that might makes right, is a realist cynic. Both types of cynic remove themselves from the real-world drama of public policy and moral decision.

The answer to the utopians and simplifiers is a multiple-consideration approach. The absolutist with a single-issue or single-answer mentality must be confronted by the concerned realist who seeks a constructive balance among many competing goals by using such tools as cost-benefit, trade-off, and marginal analysis. At what point do transfers of income to *reduce* poverty, for example, destroy incentives to work and save? In a dangerous world and in view of domestic needs, how much should we spend on national defense?

Utopianism takes several forms. Reinhold Niebuhr referred to the Marxist-Leninists as "hard utopians" because they insist on bringing heaven on earth by force and terror. Few and perhaps no American public policy groups fall into this category, though a small number are sympathizers with or apologists for the totalitarians who often operate under the banner of "liberation." The main problem in America is the "soft utopians," the romantics who believe their special cause is so just and pure that it should take precedence over conventional wisdom or consensus. The extreme environmentalists and the zero-risk champions are examples. They insist that we protect the natural environment even to the point of greatly diminishing our standard of living, that we build a car that can't hurt anyone, that we make all drugs risk-free. For psychological or philosophical reasons, these utopians are unable to accept the commonsense fact that life is finite, frail, and full of risk. Perhaps the most extreme current form of utopianism is found among those who call upon the United States to destroy its nuclear weapons unilaterally, regardless of what the Soviet Union does.

All utopian thinking neglects or underplays the factor of cost, both in material and in human terms. For instance, the cost of American unilateral disarmament may well be the enslavement of much of the world by perhaps the most brutal tyranny in history. Utopians are also prone to twist or ignore facts that do not fit their romantic notions. This form of moral and scholarly irresponsibility is widespread in the most zealous cause groups and sometimes finds its way into generally moderate single-issue organizations.

This tendency to fix on one issue, to overlook facts, and to cling to a utopian vision is illustrated in the world-wide campaign against the "neutron bomb." This "bomb" is in fact an enhanced-radiation warhead designed for tactical use against a Soviet tank assault in Western Europe. When its existence became public, a Washington reporter dubbed it a weapon that "kills people and not property" because it would kill a tank crew without destroying the tank. The characterization was picked up by Radio Moscow and peace groups, who called it an inhumane and immoral weapon.

Actually, the "neutron bomb" is more humane than the tactical nuclear arms it would replace, because the damage it causes is far more limited. The present bombs destroy the tank and its crew along with nearby battlefield troops, civilians, and civilian buildings. "Neutron bombs" are small and cause little collateral damage. Further, radiation caused by present nuclear arms is long-lasting, while radiation emitted by the "neutron bomb" dissipates quickly. In the name of morality, then, certain peace advocates have virtually prevented the deployment of a more humane weapon and a more effective deterrent to Soviet aggression. Public policy groups that similarly ignore key facts and recommend simplistic "solutions" hardly deserve the support of discerning corporations.

The Longer View and the Role of Ideas

Public policy must be concerned with long-range as well as near-range and immediate problems. But Americans, perhaps because they lack the perspective that a long national history can give, tend to be preoccupied with the present. As Daniel Boorstin says, "we have enlarged our sense of the contemporary."[7]

Responsible public policy organizations address both near-range issues and long-range political development, and the relation between the two. (Some also pay close attention to immediate legislative proposals; a prime example is the Heritage Foundation.) They tend to focus on probable or possible developments over the next ten, twenty, or even thirty years. By contrast, many activist, single-interest groups concentrate on immediate legislative and judicial issues, without considering the long-range implications.

Ideas have consequences, and ideas with values attached have even greater consequences. But ideas, however valid, require champions. Political ideas like justice and freedom need statesmen who can translate them into political structures. Economic ideas like a free market cannot come to fruition without entrepreneurs who have the inventiveness and initiative to develop them.

Business leaders, understandably occupied with keeping up with the competition and meeting a payroll, are often impatient with ideas, abstractions, and the academics who deal with them. But the survival of our society depends upon good ideas. These ideas and the institutions that cultivate them deserve support, even if the benefits are not immediate or certain. It took a long time for the ideas of Milton Friedman to be recognized and translated into policy. And the wisdom of Edmund Burke is hardly the rule in contemporary politics. The test of statesmanship and of business leadership is the capacity to see the relevance of ideas for present and future decisions and the willingness to support efforts to apply Western values to specific problems.

Relation Between Donor and Recipient

The corporate contributor and the recipient can relate to each other in various ways. Some are legitimate and constructive; others would compromise the integrity of one or both parties. The possibility of conflict of interest is inherent in any ties between two bodies seeking similar objectives.

Every tax-free corporation by law has an obligation to serve the public through charitable or educational activities. If an educational group addresses significant issues, grapples with all relevant facts, and reaches plausible conclusions, it merits support. Obviously, its data must be as objective as possible, and it must observe the rules of evidence; its conclusions must never be tailored to meet the interests or biases of any donor or other external source. No public policy group has a right to exist if it does not try assiduously to observe these elementary rules of honesty and academic integrity. But this does not mean that the conclusions resulting from its research are "objective" or value-free. Conclusions are always value-laden because they are reached by relating a premise or principle to verifiable data; they are a marriage of ethics and fact.

A responsible policy group will resist any attempt by a donor or by any other source to influence the conclusions of a research project. This does not mean, however, that there should be no contact between donor and recipient. It is both natural and desirable for the donor and the policy organization to communicate as long as the donor does not attempt to influence the outcome of an organization's research. Donors are often valuable sources of information; they can provide data on a particular topic, suggest potential audiences for publications or conferences, identify problems that need research attention, and the like.

But discerning corporations and the public policy organizations they support will observe two prudent safeguards to avoid the reality or appearance of untoward influence of donor on recipient. *First,* the organization's sources of support should be diverse—a mixture of foundations, corporations, and individuals. And corporate contributions should come from a wide range of businesses—energy, food, transportation, electronics, banking, retailing, and so on. With this varied funding, the policy group cannot be properly accused of being a spokesman for one special interest.

Second, a corporation with a direct interest in a specific project, especially if it hopes to prove a controversial point, should contract out the task to a profit-making research firm rather than to a *tax-exempt* public policy center. Private foundations are not precluded from earmarking grants for special purposes; nor are corporations—*as long as they have no direct interest in the outcome of the project.* But in no case should the interests of the source of funds dictate the conclusions.

A corporation may, of course, legitimately subsidize the publication and distribution of a report or study *after* the public policy group has reached its conclusions. To use an example close to home: an oil company may give money for the specific purpose of distributing the Ethics and Public Policy Center's study *Does Big Business Rule America?,* which argues against detailed government planning and for the market. It would be inappropriate, however, for an oil company to pay the Center to do a study such as *The Oil Muddle: Control vs. Competition,* in which James B. Ramsey concludes that the oil shortages during the late 1970s were due to U.S. government regulation and that market forces are more effective than regulation in maintaining an adequate, realistically priced supply of oil.

But would it be ethical for an oil company to make a grant to promote a wider distribution of *The Oil Muddle,* or to provide the Center with a mailing list for advertising this book? Yes, because such support relates only to the distribution of independently reached conclusions. It in no way compromises the integrity of the author or the sponsoring organization. However, what is ethical may not always be prudent. Since some critics see collusion where there is none, it may be wise to accept only general program support, not specific promotional grants, from "interested" sources.

Contract research between a corporation and a public policy group presents problems. Some policy groups have solved this by having both profit and non-profit elements. The Stanford Research Institute is an example. The Brookings Institution, the American Enterprise Institute, and most other similar organizations do not do corporate contract research, though some of their staff members serve as consultants to corporations on their own time. In matters like this, a public policy organization is more like a university than a business for profit.

Research funds from state or federal government agencies raise similar questions. Again, there is no necessary contradiction between responsiveness to the terms of the contract and the preservation of the policy group's integrity unless the group seeks to curry favor by tailoring its findings or other activities.

The ethical problems between him who gives and him who receives are age old. Pope Julius II, the patron of Michelangelo, did not control the artist's creative vision for the Sistine Chapel; on the other hand, the pope could have withheld further patronage had he been dissatisfied with the results. There may be more in common between art and political philosophy than is generally recognized. The poet and the painter do not sell their souls to their patron; nor do researchers, writers, or administrators of responsible policy organizations.

There have been occasional exceptions, as in the case of John Dryden and his patron, John Wilmot, Earl of Rochester. One evening the earl and a group of wits held a competition to decide who could write the best impromptu poem. Dryden was to judge. When the poems were in, Dryden read them and pronounced the earl the winner. The prize-winning literary effort read: "I promise to pay John Dryden 500 pounds. John Wilmot, Earl of Rochester." However, patron and client rarely trade so blatant a quid (or 500 quid) for so blatant a quo!

CHAPTER FOUR

Effectiveness Criteria

WHEN A CORPORATION DECIDES to support public policy organizations that share its political and economic goals, it may soon discover that not all groups that affirm such goals are capable of advancing them. How can corporate leaders select a few groups to support among the many with similar names and promotional brochures? Here they need to judge *effectiveness* by considering the following interrelated questions about a possible recipient.
1. Are its purpose and program well defined?
2. Does it have a reputation for quality and reliability?
3. Is it efficiently and responsibly managed?
4. Does it have a sound financial base?
5. Has it had an impact on public policy?

Some of these questions do not apply to a new policy group that is looking for seed money; here the potential donor must rely on the reputation, character, and credibility of the organizers.

1. Are Its Purpose and Program Well Defined?

A worthy public policy organization should have a constructive and socially useful reason for existence; its purposes should be clearly stated; and it should have a program that serves its central goals. Goals are easy to profess but much more difficult to achieve in a complex and difficult world where a bewildering variety of groups have similar purposes and activities.

Some existing policy groups should not have been started because their principal activity duplicates the work that others are doing. Others should not continue because their work is inferior and ineffective. The nation would be better served if policy groups were subjected more rigorously to the test of competition, so that the stronger and better would survive. The "market" would test the capacity of a proposed or existing center to secure support from the private sector (and in some cases from the government).

Clarity of purpose and program should lead to fruitful cooperation and eliminate wasteful duplication. Here the clearinghouse function of the Heritage Foundation's data bank and newsletter is important. Centers that specialize in consumer, media, energy, or foreign policy issues need especially to be aware of what others in their field are doing—both those with similar views and those with opposing views.

Yet there is also such a thing as constructive duplication. Similar organizations should welcome reinforcing, balancing, and corrective duplication that serves the cause of sound policy. It would be good, for example, if Brookings and AEI simultaneously put out studies of the oil crisis, or of the effect of the "neutron bomb" on NATO's capacity to deter a Soviet tank assault against Western Europe. And some areas of endeavor that are quite specialized nonetheless offer ample space for several similar groups. In media analysis, for instance, there is room for additional efforts to supplement the good and complementary work of the Media Institute and Accuracy in Media, both located in Washington.

Fads may be the lifeblood of the fashion world, but they are the bane of the public policy community. Suddenly a bold headline heralds a new problem and a dozen groups pounce on it, each eager to get out the first analysis. The preoccupation with the novel or immediate that is so characteristic of the news media should not be emulated by policy researchers; they should grapple with the continuing problems and focus on a more distant horizon.

2. Does It Have a Reputation for Quality and Reliability?

A good reputation is a precious asset. Unlike a good image, reputation must be earned; image can, at least to a degree, be concocted by Madison Avenue techniques. The reputation of a policy group rests on what people who matter think of it. These include peers in the non-profit and philanthropic world as well as journalists, scholars, business leaders, and policy-makers who know what the group has been doing.

The reputation of an organization is inseparable from the reputation of the people who operate it—the senior staff and, to a lesser extent, the board of directors. Are the staff respected persons of honesty and integrity? Are their opinions taken seriously by both those who share and those who oppose their public philosophy? Are their services sought by universities, other public policy groups, community organizations, and government officials? Are their ideas reported or commented on by the general press, radio, and TV? If the staff have no outlet for their views except the organization's own publications, their reputation may rest on a rather narrow base.

A profile of highly respected public policy executives or researchers would include all or some of the following features. They are in demand as speakers at universities and at national and international conferences. They appear on radio and TV public-affairs programs. Their advice is sought by Washington policymakers. Their writings appear both in specialized publications and in the general press, including publications whose editorial positions differ from theirs. They may be nominated to serve in the local, state, or federal government. This profile has been realized many times at Brookings, AEI, Heritage, the Hoover Institution, and smaller centers. An outstanding case in point is Jeane Kirkpatrick, a scholar at AEI and a member of the Board of Directors of the Ethics and Public Policy Center, who was selected by President Reagan to serve as the U.S. representative to the United Nations.

The capacity of public policy administrators or scholars to gain the respect of their opponents contributes significantly to their reputation. Attention from ideological adversaries suggests that their ideas have succeeded in hitting a sensitive target. When clarity, integrity, and force of argument make possible the penetration of an opposing camp, whether the *Wall Street Journal* or the *New York Times,* readers have an opportunity to test their own views by the debate on the editorial pages.

Other factors enhancing reputation are imagination and courage: imagination in presenting material, and courage in addressing controversial topics. Creative communication increases the audience but has little to do with the validity of the message, the late Marshall McLuhan notwithstanding.

3. Is It Efficiently and Responsibly Managed?

The great majority of public policy groups are incorporated as not-for-profit educational organizations and have an IRS classification of 501(c)(3). By charter they are required to serve the public interest and be accountable to their directors or trustees. In addition to being legally and financially accountable, the chief executive should be an efficient manager. Efficiency is less difficult to assess than effectiveness, because the output of similar organizations can be compared through fairly tangible means such as annual reports, personnel rosters, budgets, and balance sheets. Cost-benefit analysis can quickly establish that it cost Center A three times as much to research and publish a hundred-page study as it cost Center B to produce a comparable study, or that Center B with the same expenditure was reaching an audience twice as large. One of the best indicators is income from the sale of publications as percentage of expenditures. Among public policy groups this figure ranges from less than 1 per cent to more than 10 per cent. The ratio of money spent on fund-raising to funds actually raised is another useful indicator.

Figures like these must not be taken as the sole measure of efficiency, of course. The quality of the product must be fully considered. One excellent and expensive study is worth ten poor and inexpensive ones.

4. Does It Have a Sound Financial Base?

Most public policy groups must pay continued attention to fund-raising, and perhaps this is as it should be if one believes the "market" should determine the survival of the fittest. Every non-endowed center must earn its way in a highly competitive environment. Some super-centers like Brookings and AEI are partially endowed, but even these giants are faced with the necessity of soliciting funds from besieged donors.

Few policy groups have the money in hand to operate for more than six months. This is a fact of life in the non-profit world and is not necessarily a sign of financial shakiness. Far preferable to this hand-to-mouth existence, however, would be a reserve to cover a year or eighteen months of future operation. This would permit more efficient planning, including plans for further funding, and also increase assets through investment income. Corporations could advance this objective by making two- or three-year commitments to groups that have proved their worth, rather than requiring a fresh request for a contribution each year.

Every policy organization should have an independent annual audit by a certified public accountant and should be willing to make that report and other relevant financial records available to a prospective donor without violating the confidentiality due other contributors.

5. Has It Had an Impact on Public Policy?

The final test of any policy group is the effect it has on the outcome of issues it addresses. Effect analysis is always difficult because of multiple causation; we can never be sure just which straw broke the camel's back, or which weapons system deterred the Soviet Union. Every law, executive order, and judicial decision is the product of many contending forces.

It is important to distinguish between short-range and long-range impact. A policy decision in Washington arises from the current interplay of forces, but these current forces may be the result, not only of the push and shove of practical politics, but of decades of debate in the intangible realm of ideas. Consequently, the impact standard must take into account the character and objectives of a particular policy organization. A group seeking specific and immediate legislative reform should be so judged. An institution that focuses on concepts somewhat removed from current legislation or executive decisions must be assessed by its capacity to articulate those ideas in ways that enrich public debate. Policy groups engaged in critical studies of institutions (e.g., of churches, schools, trade unions, the press, or bureaucratic structures) should be judged by whether they help to make problems known and understood and whether they influence the institutions concerned.

Activist, single-issue organizations are likely to have a more visible impact than multiple-issue and more academically oriented research groups. The single-issue groups sometimes score quick victories on specific issues. By oversimplification, a highly selective use of facts, and the use of emotive slogans, zealous groups can mobilize public opinion and get results, especially on Capitol Hill. In 1981, for example, there was a lopsided vote in the House and Senate condemning the Administration for not supporting a marketing code by which the World Health Organization proposed to regulate the sale of infant formula throughout the world. In this case, the Congress was influenced by a broad-based popular pressure group, the Infant Formula Action Coalition (INFACT), while the Administration accepted the more sober assessment of the case put forward by more academic public policy groups.[1] It is far easier to get an ill-conceived law (like the Freedom of Information Act) passed than to undo the damage it subsequently causes.

The overall question is, then, does the organization effectively reach its target audience of thinkers and doers? The term "target audience" means, first, key decision-makers. The prime target in the United States is the President. Few policy groups have direct access to him, but some do have active access to top members of his staff. In the administration of President Jimmy Carter, for example, several Brookings Institution staffers were appointed to important positions. When President Reagan took over, several senior staff members of the Hoover Institution, the Heritage Foundation, and the American Enterprise Institute were given key posts.

Between the top of the decision-making pyramid and "the public" are the "opinion leaders"—the executive bureaucracy and the congressional staff, business leaders, lobbyists, academic leaders, community leaders, religious leaders, and the media. These groups are the primary target audience of most public policy organizations. At the same time, policy groups seek to reach a larger public audience for their views by enlisting the services of journalists and professors who consciously or unconsciously carry their message for them. In a democracy the support of the larger public is essential, and no responsible policy group should indulge in the elitist error of ignoring the "man in the street." In the pyramid of American society there is a flow of ideas in both directions, but ideas are generated near the top. This may seem obvious, but some people pretend to believe that in a mass democracy, ideas actually spring from "the people." Irving Kristol made this point at a National Chamber Foundation conference in 1978:

> Public opinion in the United States takes the form of a pyramid in which the flow is from the point to the base. Public opinion does not move from the base to the point. At the tip is what you might call the educated class in our society today, including the Academy, including those 600,000 professors who write the textbooks which educate your children and mine, who teach the people who go into the media. They are the ultimate source of public opinion in this country. It is popular folly to think that it can or should be otherwise....
> ... The mass media are parasitic on the Academy. The mass media know what the Academy tells them, not more, not less, and under no circumstances will the mass media, for any period of time, entertain an opinion which the Academy dismisses.[2]

An influential audience that has been largely overlooked until quite recently is religious leaders. Many people may think that the Moral Majority and other conservative religious groups "invented" religion's concern for political issues, but there has always been a close connection between religion and politics, between ethics and public policy.[3] Each age has seen these two powerful forces related in its own particular way. "Liberal" Protestants carried their social gospel to Washington and the state capitals long before the conservatives became active. For decades American Catholics have been active in church-state issues; in recent years they have greatly expanded their political agenda. Two public policy groups that have undertaken to analyze the influence of religious groups on political decisions are the Ethics and Public

Policy Center and the Institute for Religion and Democracy, both located in Washington. The Marxist-oriented Institute for Policy Studies also maintains contact with many establishment religious leaders and groups.

"Access" to a particular leadership elite implies influence, but there are many degrees of access and therefore of influence. The highest form of access is personal contact based on years of acquaintance or friendship. Here national policy groups that are located in Washington have a distinct advantage, especially if their top staff have lived and worked in the capital for some time. Perhaps the least effective form of communication is the mailing of printed material to a leader whose name has been put on the mailing list without his knowledge or consent.

Influential communication can be initiated by the opinion leader or by the policy group, but the former is usually more significant. A White House speech writer may ask a public policy staffer to prepare several paragraphs on, for example, the school voucher question or the impact of a new clean air bill. Such requests are made especially of public policy researchers who have served as consultants to political leaders or to government agencies, since they are presumed to "talk the same language" as the policymaker or to understand the arcane ways of government bureaucracies.

While impact cannot be measured with precision, questions like the following suggest some reliable indicators: Do the organization's publications and conferences reach influential leaders? Do these leaders request publications or receive them automatically? Do they or their staffs order and pay for additional copies? Is there follow-up on what they receive? Do they ask the organization's staff for further information or advice? Do they suggest a conference or invite the author to testify before a congressional committee?

Similar questions may be asked about the quality of the policy group's communication with journalists, professors, business executives, religious leaders, and the leaders of other public policy groups. What evidence is there that the organization's materials are being used? Do journalists refer to them in columns, editorials, or news reports? Do college and university faculty order publications for classroom use? Are there repeat publication orders and other initiatives from leaders who address larger audiences?

To be able to give the desirable answers to questions like these, a policy group must produce thoughtful studies, reports, proposals, periodicals, or conferences that meet a felt need. Effective communication is vital for any organization seeking to reach a diverse audience. The excessive use of abstract, academic terms or of the technical language of certain disciplines narrows the audience and turns off the general reader or listener, however intelligent he may be. That complex issues can be discussed in clear, non-technical language without oversimplifying has been amply demonstrated by thoughtful current public policy spokesmen such as Jeane Kirkpatrick, Irving Kristol, Arthur Schlesinger, Jr., Michael Novak, Thomas Sowell, Herbert Stein, George F. Will, and James Q. Wilson.

Access to national political leaders changes, of course, with the ebb and flow of power in Washington. Liberal policy groups that were influential during the Carter years do not have the same access to the Reagan administration, though their influence on Capitol Hill and in the executive branch continues. The more conservative groups like the Hoover Institution, the Heritage Foundation, AEI, the Institute for Contemporary Studies, and the Center for Strategic and International Studies have fuller access to an administration for which they helped to prepare the way.

CHAPTER FIVE

Reliable Sources of Information

AMERICAN CORPORATIONS LARGE AND SMALL will face unprecedented dangers and opportunities in the 1980s and beyond. They will be buffeted by the crosscurrents of an increasingly competitive economy at home and abroad. Success will require greater corporate inventiveness and imagination than ever before.

The corporation will continue to be the target of assorted critics in the academy, media, government, church, and many special-interest lobbies. Some critics will honestly want to improve corporate performance; others will seek to destroy the corporation, the market, and the free political institutions that sustain both. Corporations will be accused, with little discrimination, of producing shoddy and unsafe products, fouling the environment, robbing future generations of their resources, wielding inordinate power,[1] repressing Third World peoples, causing poverty and war, and generally being insensitive to human needs. They will be assailed by hostile stockholder resolutions, by boycotts, and occasionally by terrorist attacks. For the angry reformers and revolutionaries, corporations will continue to be major targets in the "enemy camp."

The corporation has probably been the most criticized and least understood institution in American society, as well as the one most hobbled by government regulation. And yet, business with all its imperfections has served the needs and interests of society more effectively in America than anywhere else.[2] This is not the place to review the burgeoning literature on the problems of the corporation or the criticism that has been met in the executive suites and board rooms with a mixture of breast beating, defiance, and genuine self-examination. It is the place to emphasize fresh opportunities for responsible private enterprise to strengthen its role as a counterpoise to excessively intrusive government and thus serve as a more productive force in sustaining a free and democratic society. It is also the place to express the hope that business leaders will become more sensitive to their actual and potential impact on the larger cause of freedom and justice.

In the coming decades, corporate America will be under increasing pressure to increase its contributions to worthy causes. The new frontier of corporate giving is in the vital and turbulent public policy arena. The purpose of this study is to encourage business leaders to enter this arena armed with confidence and critical imagination. Specifically, we encourage corporations to support responsible policy organizations whose commitment to free political and economic institutions has been demonstrated.

How to Make Responsible Decisions

When a corporation decides to become involved in public policy, to become a deliberate actor in helping to shape America's future, how can it decide what groups to support? Which groups meet the policy guidelines and effectiveness criteria discussed in chapters three and four? Until recently the corporation executive had virtually nowhere to turn for reliable information about the philosophy and performance of the growing number of policy groups. In most cases, management had no professionals on the staff to examine carefully the requests pouring in from a bewildering variety of groups.

A start was made when several larger corporations hired professionals to evaluate the requests, but most of these people were more familiar with traditional charitable appeals than with the novel requests from the emerging public policy community. Furthermore, their status in the corporate hierarchy was sometimes too low to command attention and respect at the top. This situation is gradually being corrected. As Michael Joyce of the Olin Foundation has pointed out, "There is a growing network of persons with good political judgment ripe for recruitment into corporate philanthropy. Once in place such a network would be a formidable political force in the private sector."

The sources of information on nonprofit groups normally consulted by corporate leaders are organizations such as the Better Business Bureau, the U.S. Chamber of Commerce, the National Association of Manufacturers, and the National Information Bureau. These together with a few more recent investigative organizations provide data on the financial integrity and reliability of charitable causes, but they are disinclined to comment on the political orientation or effectiveness of public policy organizations.

Recently these sources have been supplemented by three organizations established explicitly to serve as clearinghouses for vital information on policy groups. These new sources, all of which have the IRS classification 501(c)(3), focus on philosophy, personnel, program, and publications.

Most useful is the **Foundation for Public Affairs** (1220 Sixteenth Street N.W., Washington, D.C. 20036; 202-872-1750), which publishes *Public Interest Profiles*. These are short reports (four to eight pages each) on one hundred of the most important groups of varying political persuasions that attempt "to influence the public policy environment." The eleven categories of interest into which they are divided (such as public interest law and public policy research) are listed with examples in chapter one of this study. The Public Policy Research section of the 1982 volume profiles these eleven groups: American Enterprise Institute, Brookings Institution, Cato Institute, Democracy Project, Ethics and Public Policy Center, Heritage Foundation, Hoover Institution, Institute for Contemporary Studies, Institute for Policy Studies, Work in America Institute, and Worldwatch Institute.

Each profile indicates the public philosophy and specific positions of the group through quotations from its officials and from press reports on its activities. The publisher does not rate either policy or performance. To illustrate the value of this source we have reproduced the profiles of three differing consumer groups—Consumer Alert, the Center for Auto Safety, and the American Council on Science and Health—as an appendix. The Foundation keeps files on nearly two thousand other organizations besides those it profiles. Its monthly newsletter, *Policy Networks*, provides useful information on developments in the public policy field.

The **Institute for Educational Affairs** (310 Madison Avenue, New York, New York 10017; 212-687-2826) was established in 1979 by Irving Kristol and William E. Simon to make information on public policy groups available to potential donors. It does not make specific recommendations. It has a quarterly newsletter called *The IEA Report*.

In 1980 the IEA published a *Guide to Public Policy Research Organizations.* which it described as "a carefully considered, selective guide to organizations in the intellectual world that we believe private and corporate philanthropy ought to know about." The guide gives brief sketches of the following groups: American Council on Science and Health, American Enterprise Institute, *The American Spectator* (journal; Bloomington, Indiana), Center for Research in Government Policy and Business, Center for the Study of American Business, *Character* (journal; Chicago), *Encounter* (journal; London, England), Ethics and Public Policy Center, Heritage Foundation, Hoover Institution, Hudson Institute, Institute for Contemporary Studies, Emory University Law and Economics Center, National Bureau of Economic Research, and Public Research Syndicated.

The **Heritage Foundation** (513 C Street N.E., Washington, D.C. 20002; 202-546-4400) not only is a research and dissemination center with an impressive output but also serves as a clearinghouse for information on public policy organizations. Its Resource Bank has material on some 450 organizations. The Resource Bank issues a monthly *Insider Newsletter* reporting on publications and activities of public policy organizations. A yearly survey is published under the title *Annual Insider*.

Included in the Resource Bank are an "Academic Bank" of more than a thousand academics who are available to write, speak, and testify in their various fields of expertise, and a "Talent Bank" for bringing likeminded job applicants and employers together. The first *Annual Guide to Public Policy Experts*, published in 1982, lists some 600 specialists in various fields of domestic and foreign policy.

Besides consulting these national business associations and clearinghouses, corporation officers make use of a kind of informal network of communication that includes their counterparts in other firms, acquaintances in compatible foundations, and executives of public policy groups they have come to respect. This network has been nourished by a number of idea brokers who facilitate communication among business leaders, foundations, and public policy groups. Among these idea brokers, Frank Barnett, Michael Joyce, Irving Kristol, Richard Larry, Philip Marcus, Dan McMichael, and Michael Novak deserve special mention.

The Impact of Good Ideas

If we want democratic capitalism and democracy itself to survive the assaults of totalitarians from outside and of romantics and revolutionaries from within, we must acknowledge the shortcomings of our economic system, and at the same time combat both a false sense of guilt about our success and the utopian illusions of perfection that motivate our adversaries. The survival of responsible American corporations is a concern of us all. A free market is not unrelated to freedom of choice at the ballot box and all the other freedoms that, exercised with responsibility, add up to a democratic society. Business, academic, religious, and political leaders who are committed to the survival of these freedoms are thus inescapably involved in the war of ideas.

"The leverage of ideas," says Irving Kristol, "is so immense that a slight change in the intellectual climate can and will—perhaps slowly, but nevertheless inexorably—twist a familiar institution into an unrecognizable shape." Since the mid-1960s we have seen a number of institutions bending under the influence of bad ideas or half truths. At the same time, we have witnessed the beneficial impact of good ideas. It is precisely in this arena of struggle between good and bad ideas that public policy groups make their greatest contribution.

APPENDIX

Profiles of Three Consumer Organizations

The following sketches of Consumer Alert, the Center for Auto Safety, and the American Council on Science and Health are reprinted with permission from "Public Interest Profiles," published by the Foundation for Public Affairs (1220 Sixteenth Street N.W., Washington, D.C. 20036) in July 1982. They illustrate the value of the "Profiles." They also provide a comparison of three consumer groups that vary in size, program, and perspective.

Consumer Alert

1024 J Street
Room 425
Modesto, California 95354
(209) 524-1738

STAFF SIZE:
Consumer Alert recently moved its headquarters to Modesto, California, from Connecticut, and is in the process of rebuilding its staff. The eventual number of paid personnel will be determined by the level of contributions. At the present time, CA is utilizing the services of volunteers.

BUDGET:
$60,000 in 1981; $102,000 is proposed for 1982.

DIRECTOR:
Barbara Keating-Edh, president. Ms. Keating-Edh was the New York Conservative Party's candidate for the U.S. Senate in 1974. After her defeat, Ms. Keating-Edh served as a special assistant to Sen. James Buckley, R-N.Y. While still serving as president of Consumer Alert, she headed the Reagan transition team at the Consumer Product Safety Commission.

SCOPE:
Consumer Alert is a national, nonprofit organization with over 5,000 members. Members can be found in every state, and CA's primary interest is national consumer issues.

PURPOSE:

CA seeks "to advance the consumer interest through advocacy of free-market solutions to consumer dissatisfaction and scrutiny of any action which discourages competition in the marketplace."

CA is a 501(c)(3) organization, and contributions to it are tax-deductible.

METHOD OF OPERATION:

(1) *Research and Publications:* CA has conducted a number of surveys on consumer attitudes toward government regulation. Some of these polls were taken within CA's membership, and some involved the public at large. CA has polled motorists on passive restraint safety systems; children on the effects of television advertisements upon eating habits; and the general public on attitudes toward the use of nitrites in cured meat products, factors involved in furniture and gasoline purchases, and experiences with microwave ovens.

CA occasionally publishes brochures detailing the results of its surveys. The group also issues copies of testimony given by staff members and periodic "Tip Sheets" for consumers.

(2) *Testimony:* "CA is often invited to give its opinion regarding proposed or existing regulations and laws." For example, in 1980, CA submitted comments to the Food and Drug Administration opposing proposed revisions in food labeling and mandatory patient package inserts for prescription drugs. CA testified before the House Subcommittee on Antitrust and Restraint of Trade Matters on retail divorcement and before the New York and Maryland state legislatures on mandatory bottle deposits. In a letter to Secretary of Transportation Drew Lewis, CA supported a petition filed by the Pacific Legal Foundation urging reconsideration and repeal of passive auto restraints. CA also testified on passive auto restraints before the National Highway Traffic Safety Administration.

During 1981, CA submitted comments to the Senate Banking Committee favoring a bill deregulating interest rates on consumer loans.

(3) *Litigation:* Beginning in 1979, CA was involved in a cooperative suit with the Mid-Atlantic Legal Foundation involving the payment of mandatory fees by Rutgers University students to the New Jersey Public Interest Research Group. The U.S. District Court in New Jersey ruled against CA's position and in favor of continued mandatory fees on June 19, 1981. CA continues to press this issue in the court of appeals.

In 1981, CA joined in a suit filed by the Pacific Legal Foundation in the California Superior Lower Court against the Abalone Alliance. The suit seeks damages of $1 million for costs incurred by the State of California and by the County of San Luis Obispo in maintaining order and protecting property during demonstrations at the Diablo Canyon nuclear facility.

In 1982, CA and the Pacific Legal Foundation intervened in the U.S. Court of Appeals in support of the Department of Transportation's decision to delay passive restraint requirements in automobiles.

(4) *Public Education:* CA collects films, articles, books and other materials for

use by teachers in prompting classroom discussion of consumer and environmental issues. It sponsors lectures for schools and for community, trade, and consumer groups on the consumer movement. CA also distributes brochures on various consumer topics.

In 1980, Ms. Keating-Edh was a cofounder, with the Heritage Foundation, of the National Coalition for Growth. The Coalition sponsors "Growth Day," initially held in response to "Big Business Day." The Coalition believes that, "America's commitment to expanding opportunity for every citizen depends on continued economic growth, which in turn depends primarily on the collective business enterprise."

NEWSLETTER:
Consumer Comments, a bimonthly newsletter for members, is available to corporations for $50 per year. Corporations may also receive the newsletter and all press releases for $125 annually, or the newsletter, press releases, and CA testimony for $250 per year. Individual membership dues are $20 annually.

HISTORY:
Consumer Alert, Inc., was organized in May 1977 by August G. Fromuth and Barbara Keating through a $50,000 bank loan guaranteed by the Precision Valve Corporation. During the past three years, CA's membership has remained relatively constant at approximately 5,000 members; its budget has declined slightly from 1979-1980 levels. CA was originally located in Darien, Connecticut. The group opened a California office in 1980, and shifted its headquarters to Modesto, California in 1981.

BOARD OF DIRECTORS:
Members of CA's board of directors "serve a three-year renewable term and are expected to attend Board meetings on a regular basis." Officers are John Sununu, chairman; Fred Turek, vice chairman and secretary; and Arthur J. Finkelstein, treasurer. The remaining members of the board are N. Richard Greenfield, Barbara Keating-Edh, Frank L. McHugh, and Anthony P. Palladino.

Consumer Alert also has a 21-member advisory council:

Petr Beckmann	Tex McCrary
Yale Brozen	H. Peter Metzger
Roland T. Bryan	J. A. Parker
Taylor Caldwell	H. Daniel Roth
Joseph A. Cimino	William E. Simon
Milton Copulos	Richard O. Simpson
Edith Efron	Leonard J. Theberge
Arthur Godfrey	Gloria E. A. Toote
David P. Harmon	I. W. Tucker
Reed Irvine	Elizabeth Whelan
Thomas H. Jukes	

FUNDING:
One-third of Consumer Alert's income is from membership dues, subscriptions, and individual contributions. Another third comes from corporate contributions and subscriptions, and the remainder from private foundations. Contributions are accepted for general operation only, and "no government funding is sought or accepted."

Among the foundation contributors during 1980 were The Wappler Foundation, John M. Olin Foundation, Northwest Industries Foundation, The Procter & Gamble Fund, The Continental Group Foundation, and the Adolph Coors Foundation.

EFFECTIVENESS:
CA has been effective in meeting its goal of establishing "an alternative voice within the consumer movement." Ms. Keating-Edh's opinions on consumer issues are frequently cited by the media, and CA is often called to comment at agency and legislative proceedings.

CA is sometimes criticized as a "front for industry" by other consumer groups. The group is viewed as influential by the Reagan administration, however, as evidenced by Ms. Keating-Edh's participation on the transition team. CA's budget and membership levels have not grown appreciably in the past few years.

POLITICAL ORIENTATION:
Consumer Alert offers this description of the proper role of consumer advocacy: "Business can best serve consumers by providing quality products at competing prices. One can assume that anything which interferes with the voluntary interaction between competing producers and discerning shoppers should be avoided. True consumer advocacy must consistently oppose any activity prompted by government or industry which seeks to reduce competitiveness."

Consumer Alert generally opposes those measures backed by other consumer groups which involve increased government regulation. A 1980 article by Caroline E. Mayer in the *Washington Star* noted that Ms. Keating-Edh "earned her reputation by heading a consumer organization that more often than not oppose[s] the policies of most well-known consumer groups." *The New Right Report* described Consumer Alert as "the Right's answer to Ralph Nader."

In a speech at Hillsdale College, Ms. Keating-Edh made this appraisal of the current consumer movement: "The no-growth movement playing havoc with our freedoms today gains momentum by fanning public paranoia and doting on those persons who can't be happy unless they believe they are being poisoned by someone who is earning a profit. . . .

"The examples in which consumers are being ripped off by 'their own' movement are legion. I have concluded that no greater threat exists to individual liberty than those restrictions placed upon each of us in the name of consumer protection."

FUTURE AGENDA:
"Consumer Alert is contemplating . . . a feasibility study aimed at alternative ways of delivering first class mail." The group believes that "competition in mail delivery is essential if the system is to be cost efficient." CA is also conducting a comprehensive survey of its members to determine their opinions on energy issues.

Center For Auto Safety
1223 Dupont Circle Building
Washington, D.C. 20036
(202) 659-1126

STAFF SIZE:
15 staff members; 12 professional, 3 support.

DIRECTOR:
Clarence M. Ditlow, III, executive director. Mr. Ditlow was formerly with Ralph Nader's Public Interest Research Group.

BUDGET:
$250,000 in 1981; $300,000 is proposed for 1982.

SCOPE:
The Center for Auto Safety is a Washington-based research, litigation, and advocacy organization concerned with vehicle and highway safety. CFAS has over 3,000 members, and handles approximately 30,000 auto complaints every year.

PURPOSE:
"The Center for Auto Safety is a nonprofit public interest organization established to promote reduced deaths and injuries from motor vehicles and highways."
  CFAS is a 501(c)(3) organization, and contributions to it are tax-deductible.

METHOD OF OPERATION:
  (1) *Agency Monitoring and Testimony:* CFAS frequently testifies before federal agencies on issues related to automobile and highway safety. During 1981, CFAS opposed efforts by the National Highway Traffic Safety Administration (NHTSA) to weaken automobile bumper standards. CFAS testified before NHTSA on delays in passive restraint requirements, claiming that "one need only look at the automobile companies' price estimates for air bags to see that they are still peddling that same old baloney to the American public."

In a letter to the assistant attorney general for antitrust, CFAS protested a Justice Department decision to allow auto companies to exchange technical information on emission controls. The Center criticized the relaxing of 1983 Environmental Protection Agency (EPA) pollution standards for trucks and heavy-duty vehicles, and testified before the Federal Highway Administration on a rule involving the use of federal funds for repair of noninterstate highways.

CFAS also filed petitions with the Federal Trade Commission (FTC) on a number of nonsafety defects. Successful efforts in this area included FTC rulings on Ford engines, Volkswagen diesel engine failures, and Honda rust problems. Petitions still under investigation involve General Motors Type 200 transmissions, Volkswagen oil consumption, and General Motors diesel engines.

(2) *Public Education:* A major function of CFAS is to inform the public, often through open letters to federal agencies, of what it perceives to be product defects, warranty deficiencies, agency inaction, and corporate collusion.

During 1981, CFAS criticized Ford and Chrysler for ceasing to issue public notices of car recalls. The Center also made public an internal NHTSA document citing "confidential" cost estimates by Ford and General Motors for airbags. These estimates were considerably less than figures publicly available, and CFAS has been ordered to return the document, under threat of criminal action. CFAS also claimed that the Department of Transportation (DOT) concealed a study by Opinion Research Corporation which indicated a high level of effectiveness for automatic seat belts.

(3) *Litigation:* CFAS initiates law suits—often in conjunction with public interest law organizations—aimed at forcing regulatory agency compliance or industry disclosure. During 1981, the Center and four other consumer groups sued NHTSA to force a recall of Ford cars with transmissions that reportedly jump from park to reverse. In October 1981 the suit was rejected by a federal judge, although CFAS has appealed the decision. Another CFAS suit against NHTSA involved the agency's revocation of safety standards regulating fields of direct view in passenger cars.

CFAS took action to block a Department of Transportation attempt to postpone passive restraint requirements. The Center also sued the Department of Justice to keep in effect a consent decree prohibiting car makers from taking joint positions on emission standards.

CFAS conducted a "Lemon Law Litigation Conference" during March 1981. The conference, attended by 200 trial lawyers, was designed to show "how to select and assemble successful warranty suits, under the Magnuson-Moss Warranty Act, against manufacturers or dealers of defective or unsafe vehicles—lemons."

As part of its efforts to encourage "lemon litigation," CFAS has recently begun publication of *The Lemon File*. This quarterly publication covers auto warranty cases from state and federal courts across the nation. It also provides "up-to-date case profiles, a detailed index, a lawyer referral index, listings of widespread defects suitable for joinder and class actions, listings of auto defects currently under investigation by NHTSA and recent recall data."

(4) *Research and Publications:* Although CFAS does not address individual complaints, the Center collects information and monitors consumer opinion on vehicle/product safety and reliability, and on issues related to safe highway construction. CFAS has released seven books, including *The Lemon Book* and *Litigation Manual on the Magnuson-Moss Warranty Act.* The Center has also published 31 reports and statements. Recent Center reports have addressed highway safety, recreational vehicles, and Volkswagen Rabbit oil consumption. In 1981, the Center assisted in the independent publication of *The Car Book,* formerly published by NHTSA.

CFAS also assembles consumer information and litigation packages on specific issues. Consumer information packets released during 1981 included materials on Ford transmission defects, passive restraints, highway resurfacing, and automobile warranties. The Center has accumulated information on seven major lawsuits, including two 1981 lawsuits against the Department of Transportation involving Ford transmissions and passive restraint delays.

NEWSLETTER:
IMPACT, a bimonthly newsletter, is available by subscription for $35 per year. *The Lemon Times* is published quarterly for $15 per year.

HISTORY:
"The Center for Auto Safety was established in 1970 by Ralph Nader and Consumers Union. From the outset, the Center has concentrated on highway safety and has worked closely with Ralph Nader. But the scope of the issues the Center addresses and the range of the strategies it utilizes have grown considerably.... It became independent of its founders in 1973."

CFAS is perhaps best known for its action manual for owners of "lemon" automobiles; its attempts to have Ford cars with faulty transmissions recalled; and its successful efforts which resulted in Firestone ultimately recalling nearly 18 million steel belted radial tires, at a cost of nearly $200 million.

BOARD OF DIRECTORS:
Members of the Center's board are: Edward Cohen, Hon. Bob Eckhardt, James Fitzpatrick, Benjamin Kelley, Rep. Benjamin Rosenthal (D-N.Y.), and Donald Schwartz.

FUNDING:
Primary support for CFAS comes from foundations, 50 percent; memberships, 25 percent; and publications and research, 25 percent. *National Journal* reported small grants from the federal government of $8,000 in 1981 and $3,000 in 1982. Recent foundation grants have ranged from $10,000 to $100,000. Among

CFAS's major contributors are the State Farm Insurance Foundation and the Allstate Foundation.

EFFECTIVENESS:
CFAS is widely recognized as a very effective consumer organization. The *Washington Post* described the Center as the "consumer group largely responsible for alerting the government to problems with the [Firestone] 500." The Center has been influential in other areas as well, especially with respect to mobile homes and other auto defect issues. Although Center efforts to have Ford automobiles with faulty transmissions recalled have been largely unsuccessful, CFAS has been effective in bringing the matter to public attention.

In February 1980 the *Wall Street Journal* criticized CFAS as one of a "spate of private bureaucracies . . . now earning a living by representing 'the public interest' in FTC proceedings." At this time, however, federal funding is actually minimal and is being phased out.

An analysis of *The Lemon Book* in the Summer 1981 *Business and Society Review* criticized the authors for "approaching their task with a cynicism not altogether unlike that which has too often characterized the automobile industry." The *Review* also noted, though, that the book's "heart is in the right place," and despite its weaknesses, has "considerable value."

POLITICAL ORIENTATION:
CFAS often opposes corporate positions, particularly those of the automobile companies. However, the insurance industry has been supportive of some CFAS activities. In an interview in *Consumer Affairs Letter,* Clarence Ditlow outlined his position on government regulation: "In the area of health and safety, you must have government regulation. A concentrated industry like the U.S. auto industry is simply not going to offer significant health and safety features. If we were dealing with a really competitive industry and a good information system—which we don't have in the auto industry—you might be able to make a case for corporate self-regulation."

CFAS is not a partisan political organization, as disagreements with the NHTSA under both Democratic and Republican administrations have indicated.

FUTURE AGENDA:
CFAS will place greater emphasis on educating attorneys in the use of the Magnuson-Moss Warranty Act and other legal tools for assisting consumers. The Center will also encourage the increased use of class action suits to force compensation for automobile defects. CFAS will defend "auto safety and quality standards against Reagan administration attempted rollbacks," and will continue its efforts to obtain passive restraints in all passenger automobiles. A December 1981 article in the *Washington Post* indicated that the Center may shift the focus of its battle for passive restraints to the state level.

American Council on Science and Health

1995 Broadway
18th Floor
New York, New York 10023
(212) 362-7044

1111 19th Street N.W.
Suite 301
Washington, D.C. 20036
(202) 659-8978

STAFF SIZE:
13 staff members; 9 professional, 4 support.

BUDGET:
$761,000 in 1981; $1 million is proposed for 1982.

DIRECTOR:
Elizabeth M. Whelan, executive director. Dr. Whelan has been executive director of the Council since its formation in 1978, and was previously a research associate at the Harvard School of Public Health. She received her education from Connecticut College, Yale School of Medicine, and the Harvard School of Public Health.

SCOPE:
"The American Council on Science and Health is a national association of scientists from a variety of disciplines." ACSH has approximately 4,000 members and 155 supporters. It has offices in New York and Washington, D.C., and a membership office at 47 Maple Street, Summit, New Jersey 07901.

PURPOSE:
"The American Council on Science and Health brings to consumers and policymakers the most reliable conclusions to be drawn from respected research on nutritional and environmental questions as they relate to human health. Wise personal decisions and sound public health policies require consideration of the findings of scientific investigation as well as the lessons of experience, frequently called common sense."

ACSH is a 501(c)(3) organization, and contributions to it are tax-deductible.

METHOD OF OPERATION:

(1) *Research and Publications:* "The American Council achieves its purpose by publishing detailed reports on the health risks and benefits associated with public health and environmental issues that confront our society. These position papers are based on extensive reviews of the most current and relevant literature on a specific topic, and supplemented by consultations with leading specialists from the fields of public health, medicine, nutrition, and the environmental sciences.

"The American Council's areas of interest are wide-ranging. These include such popular concerns as food additives, nutrition, drugs, pesticides, environmental pollution, and regulatory legislation."

54 APPENDIX

Among the scientific reports released by ACSH during 1981-82 were: *Air Pollution and Your Health; Vitamin B-15; Anatomy of a Health Fraud; The Health Effects of Herbicide 2,4,5,-T; The Health Effects of Caffeine; Fast Food and the American Diet; Diet Modification: Can It Reduce the Risk of Heart Disease?; Alcohol Use During Pregnancy;* and *Wood as Home Fuel: A Source of Air Pollution.* In addition, the Council has released updates of previous reports on food additives and hyperactivity, cancer in New Jersey, and saccharin.

The Council also communicates its research results through a bimonthly newsletter, *ACSH News and Views.* Major articles in the newsletter during 1981 addressed such issues as unwarranted regulatory actions, factors in the decision to ban DDT, mail-order health-product advertisements, and the government's reaction to a controversial report on cholesterol.

Books published by Council scientists during 1981 included: *The Food Additives Dictionary,* by Dr. Melvin Benarde; *Vitamins and "Health" Foods—The Great American Hustle,* by Dr. Victor Herbert and Stephen Barrett; and *No Need for Hunger,* by Dr. Robert R. Spitzer.

(2) *Public Education:* ACSH conducts an ambitious program to communicate its research results to the media and the general public. For example, during 1981, the Council held press conferences in New York and Washington to release its reports on air pollution, caffeine, and the herbicide 2,4,5,-T.

In September 1981 ACSH initiated a syndicated newspaper column, "Focus on Science and Health," for use in newspapers across the country. The column "provides consumers with factual, common-sense information on a wide variety of health topics—some of them quite controversial." Fees from the syndication will go toward the formation of an ACSH scholarship fund for students of public health and nutrition.

In March 1982 ACSH began distribution of a series of 90-second radio commentaries on current health topics. The goal of the series "is to counteract many fallacious beliefs currently held as 'truths' by the public about nutrition, environmental chemicals, and human health."

(3) *Testimony:* Council staff members occasionally testify before Congress and regulatory agencies on important issues. For example, during 1980, ACSH testified on diet and heart disease and on nitrite and food safety. During 1981, ACSH directors participated in numerous Food and Drug Administration conferences, including those which focused on sodium labeling of food and on changes in food safety laws.

(4) *Awards:* In December 1981 the Council conducted its first annual awards reception. "The ACSH Award is given in recognition of unique professional achievement in the field of science or medicine which has furthered understanding of the relationship of chemicals, nutrition, and the environment to human health." The 1981 winner was Dr. John Higginson, founding director of the World Health Organization's International Agency for Research on Cancer.

NEWSLETTER:
Inside ACSH, a quarterly newsletter, is available upon request.

HISTORY:
"During the 1970s a number of U.S. scientists became concerned that important public policies related to health and the environment were being established in quite unscientific ways. The dominant voices in debates over cancer, nutrition, pollution, and food safety were often political and emotional.

"In 1978 a group of these scientists formed the American Council on Science and Health. Their aim was to increase the scientific input into health-related decision-making." The Sarah Scaife Foundation provided an initial grant of $100,000 to help establish the Council.

BOARD OF DIRECTORS:
Members of the Council's board of directors are:

Melvin A. Benarde   Joseph F. Murphy
Norman E. Borlaug   Robert E. Olson
E.M. Foster   Frederick J. Stare
Thomas H. Jukes   Elizabeth M. Whelan

ACSH also has a 62-member board of scientific advisors.

FUNDING:
Primary sources of funding for ACSH during 1981 were: unrestricted contributions, 85 percent; membership dues, 7 percent; dividends and interest, 3 percent; project fees, 3 percent; and subscription income, 2 percent. Annual membership rates for ACSH are $35 for individuals and $175 for institutions.

"Prior to September 30, 1980, ACSH did not seek or receive contributions from food, chemical, or pharmaceutical companies. After that date, ACSH's funding policy became an open one. . . .

"As of May 1981, some 5 percent of ACSH's total support came from companies and company foundations in the pharmaceutical industry; and 22 percent from diversified companies and company foundations in petrochemical related activities. Over 70 percent of ACSH's total funding comes from private foundations, individuals, and corporations with no direct financial interest in the topics ACSH investigates."

EFFECTIVENESS:
In a relatively short period of time, ACSH has become an important participant in national debates on food and drug safety. The Council's budget has increased dramatically since its formation in 1978. The Council's studies receive excellent media coverage; over 250 major newspapers and television stations covered ACSH reports during 1981. In addition, during 1981, ACSH articles and reports were accepted in a number of major magazines, including *Harper's Bazaar, Reason, Across the Board, American Baby,* and *Reader's Digest.*

Most criticisms of ACSH stem from its funding sources. In June 1981 Bob Goligoski noted in the *San Jose News* that because "of its financial ties to industry, the Council has occasionally been pelted by critics." Michael Jacobson of the Center for Science in the Public Interest has been a detractor of the Council since its inception. According to *In These Times*, Mr. Jacobson offered this opinion in early 1982: "While reasonable scientists can reasonably disagree, ACSH is using a slick scientific veneer to obscure and deny truths that virtually everyone else agrees with."

The Progressive commented similarly in April, 1982:

"Together with a sixty-two member advisory board packed with consultants to the food, drug, and chemical industries, [Elizabeth] Whelan and [Frederick] Stare have twisted the term 'consumer advocate' into a pretzel, exonerating the controversial herbicide 2,4,5-T, blaming tooth decay on the kind of sugar found in dried fruit while opposing removal of sugary 'fun food' from school cafeterias, recommending that air pollution standards be relaxed, pooh-poohing the hazards of saccharin and caffeine."

In September 1981, ACSH Executive Director Elizabeth Whelan commented on the group's funding sources:

"The funding issue will always be there in some circles if for no other reason than because it is far simpler for a critic to attempt to dismiss your views on the basis of your financial support than it is for him to grasp and critique effectively your facts and reasoning. . . .

"If we are to have a truly open dialogue in this country about controversial environmental and health issues, all views should be heard and evaluated on the basis of their merits—not their funding."

POLITICAL ORIENTATION:

ACSH notes that it was formed "to identify and oppose the pseudo-science and quackery frequently employed in pursuit of narrow objectives promoted in the name of health." As an interest group which often opposes government "over-regulation," ACSH usually works more effectively with conservative groups than with liberal organizations.

In the May 1982 issue of *Reason,* Elizabeth Whelan and Kathleen Meister offered these observations on government regulation:

"It's becoming a habit. A government agency performs or commissions a scientific study designed to answer questions about the possible health effects of a substance. The results seem to indicate a hazard. An immediate announcement is made. The news media publicize it extensively, greatly alarming the affected individuals. The agency establishes policies or takes regulatory action. Later, independent experts examine the report and find the original conclusion was in error. The study was insufficient, flawed, or misinterpreted.

"Incidents of this type have occurred all too frequently in the last few years. It would be reassuring if only trivial decisions were affected, or if a single regulatory agency were involved. But . . . this is not true. Government reliance on studies later discredited by the scientific community has become commonplace."

FUTURE AGENDA:

ACSH will continue many of its current projects and issue priorities.

Notes

CHAPTER ONE

1. *New York Times,* January 12, 1977.
2. Frances FitzGerald, *America Revised: History Schoolbooks in the Twentieth Century* (New York: Vintage Books, 1980), p. 110.
3. Ibid., p. 107.
4. *Trustees of Dartmouth College* v. *Woodward,* 4 Wheaton 518 (1819).
5. See David Kelley, "Corporate Advocacy Ads Should be Stouthearted," *Competition,* June 1981, pp. 5 and 7. For examples of advocacy advertising, see Mobil, "The U.S. stake in Middle East peace: new opportunities," *New York Times,* August 27, 1981, and "A bridge between worlds," *New York Times,* September 3, 1981. See also United Technologies, "Does the Punishment Fit the Crime?," *Wall Street Journal,* September 17, 1981.
6. Michael Killian and Arnold Sawislak, *Who Runs Washington?* (New York: St. Martin's, 1982), p. 142.
7. Federal Election Commission, "Final PAC Report for 1979-80 Election Cycle," February 21, 1982. See also Norman C. Miller, "The Political Danger of New Mega-Corporations," *Wall Street Journal,* August 20, 1981. A striking comment on the proliferation of PACs will be found in the *Washington Post,* March 30, 1982, article by Paul Taylor.
8. David Rogers, "Oil Emerges as Leading Hill Patron," *Washington Post,* September 15, 1981.
9. *First National Bank* v. *Belotti,* 435 U.S. 765. See Roger Pilon, "Corporations and Rights: On Treating Corporate People Justly," *Georgia Law Review,* Vol. 13, 1979, p. 1323, footnote. Pilon refers to a comment on the case in *Time,* May 8, 1978, p. 68.
10. Gene I. Maeroff, "Exxon Foundation Giving Schools Aid," *New York Times,* September 18, 1981.
11. Foundation for Public Affairs (Washington, D.C.), *Public Interest Profiles,* 1982.
12. David Packard, "Address to the Stanford University Alumni Association," 1974.

13. William E. Simon, "Special Address," in *What Direction? Corporate Philanthropy* (Washington: National Chamber Foundation, 1978), pp. 22-25.

14. Irving Kristol, "On Corporate Philanthropy," *Wall Street Journal,* March 21, 1977.

15. C. Lowell Harriss, "Corporate Giving: Rationale and Issues," in *Two Essays on Corporate Philanthropy and Economic Education* (New York: International Institute for Economic Research, 1977), p. 11.

16. W. Allen Wallis, "Corporate Contributions" (paper delivered at a conference sponsored by the National Association of Manufacturers, National Federation of Independent Businesses, and Foundation for Research in Economics and Education, August 1977; printed in the conference proceedings).

17. Michael Novak, *The American Vision: An Essay on the Future of Democratic Capitalism* (Washington: American Enterprise Institute, 1978), p. 48.

18. See Peter L. Berger, "Ethics and the Present Class Struggle," *Worldview,* April 1978; reprinted as *Ethics and the New Class* by the Ethics and Public Policy Center.

19. Novak, *The American Vision,* p. 53.

Chapter Two

1. Most of these facts about turn-of-the-century private philanthropy are from Daniel J. Boorstin, *The Americans: The Democratic Experience* (New York: Random House, 1973), pp. 320, 489.

2. F. Emerson Andrews, *Corporation Giving* (New York: Russell Sage Foundation, 1952), p. 28.

3. Marion R. Fremont-Smith, *Philanthropy and the Business Corporation* (New York: Russell Sage Foundation, 1972), p. 15.

4. Ibid., pp. 10-11.

5. W. Allen Wallis, "Corporate Contributions" (paper delivered at a conference sponsored by the National Association of Manufacturers, National Federation of Independent Businesses, and Foundation for Research in Economics and Education, August 1977; printed in the conference proceedings).

6. Lee Smith, "The Unsentimental Corporate Giver," *Fortune,* September 21, 1981, pp. 123-24.

7. The corporation is Berkshire Hathaway, whose chairman is Warren E. Buffett. See Lee Smith, "Shareholders Get to Vote on Charity," *Fortune,* November 30, 1981, and letter from Marcus Cohn, *Wall Street Journal,* February 17, 1982.

8. *Images of Giving: A 1979 Report on the Socially Responsive Activities of Aetna Life and Casualty Company and Aetna Life and Casualty Foundation, Inc.* (Hartford: Aetna Life and Casualty Company, 1980), pp. 17-18.

9. Professor John Holcomb of the University of Maryland writes: "According to the Conable Amendment to the 1976 Tax Reform Act, tax-exempt organiza-

tions may use up to 20 per cent of their income for lobbying purposes. Actually, a sliding scale is used with the percentage allowable declining as the organization budget increases."

10. *Giving U.S.A.* (New York: American Association of Fund-Raising Counsel, 1980), p. 18.

Chapter Three

1. John M. McGuire and Thomas W. Fletcher, "The Emerging Public Role of the Corporation," *SRI International Business Intelligence Paper,* September 1978, p. 21. See also Frank Koch, *The New Corporate Philanthropy* (New York: Plenum Press, 1979), p. 15.

2. James F. Harris and Anne Klepper, *Corporate Philanthropic Public Service Activities* (New York: The Conference Board, 1976), p. 52.

3. Irving Kristol, "On Corporate Philanthropy," *Wall Street Journal,* March 21, 1977.

4. Quoted in Clifton Fadiman, ed., *The American Treasury, 1455-1955* (New York: Harper, 1955), p. 702.

5. On corporate support for Ralph Nader see Caroline E. Mayer, "Nader, Imitating Fat Cats, to Hold Big Fund-Raiser," *Washington Post,* September 1, 1981. "Two hundred corporations were also invited, but they are only those that supported Nader's unsuccessful campaign to get Congress to pass legislation creating a Consumer Protection Agency. These companies include Montgomery Ward, Drug Fair, Giant Food, Levi Strauss, and Hallmark Cards."

6. *National Review,* October 2, 1981, p. 1116.

7. Daniel J. Boorstin, *The Exploring Spirit: America and the World, Then and Now* (New York: Vintage Books, 1977), p. 69.

Chapter Four

1. For background on this issue see: John A. Sparks, *The Nestle Controversy—Anatomy of a Boycott* (Grove City, Pa.: Public Policy Education Fund, 1980); Ernest W. Lefever, "Politics and Baby Formula in the Third World," *Wall Street Journal*, January 14, 1981; Carol Adelman, "Saving Babies With a Signature," *Wall Street Journal*, July 28, 1982.

2. Irving Kristol, "The Changing Role of Corporate Philanthropy," in *What Direction? Corporate Philanthropy* (Washington: National Chamber Foundation, 1978), p. 10.

3. See Paul J. Weber, "Examining the Religious Lobbies," *This World,* Winter/Spring 1982, pp. 97-107. Professor Weber counts 74 active religious interest groups in Washington, of which 34 are politically conservative, 29 politically liberal, 4 "mixed," and 7 not classifiable in political categories.

Chapter Five

1. See Robert Hessen, ed., *Does Big Business Rule America? Critical Commentaries on Charles E. Lindblom's 'Politics and Markets'* (Washington: Ethics and Public Policy Center, 1981).

2. See Paul Johnson, "Has Capitalism a Future?," in Ernest W. Lefever, ed., *Will Capitalism Survive? A Challenge by Paul Johnson With Twelve Responses* (Washington: Ethics and Public Policy Center, 1979).

Index of Names

Accuracy in Media, 8, 31
Aetna Life and Casualty Company, 18
Alcoa, 21
American Council on Education, 10
American Council on Science and Health, 42
American Enterprise Institute (AEI), 9, 29, 31-32, 34-35, 38, 41-42
American Political Science Association, 23
American Security Council, 9
Americans for Energy Independence, 8
American Spectator, The, 42
American Telephone and Telegraph (AT&T), 5
Amnesty International, 8
Annual Guide to Public Policy Experts (Heritage Foundation), 43
Annual Insider (Heritage Foundation), 42
A. P. Smith Manufacturing Company v. Barlow, 15
Armour Institute of Technology, 13
Armour, Philip Danforth, 13

Barnett, Frank, 43
Beard, Charles, 3
Beard, Mary, 3
Better Business Bureau, 41
Boorstin, Daniel, 26
Boy Scouts, 7
Brookings Institution, 8-9, 13, 29, 31-32, 34-35, 41
Brookings, Robert S., 13
Burke, Edmund, 27

Carnegie, Andrew, 13
Carnegie Endowment for International Peace, 14
Carnegie Foundation, 14
Carnegie Foundation for the Advancement of Teaching, 13
Carnegie Institution, 13-14
Carter, Jimmy, 35, 38
Catholic Church, 36

Cato Institute, 41
Center for Auto Safety, 8, 42
Center for Community Change, 8
Center for Defense Information, 9
Center for Law and Social Policy, 9
Center for Research in Government Policy and Business, 42
Center for Strategic and International Studies, 38
Center for the Study of American Business, 42
Chamber of Commerce, U.S., 6, 41
Character, 42
Chase Manhattan Bank, 6
Chicago, University of, 13
Church Peace Union, 14
Citizen's Choice, 8
Columbia University, 11
Commission on Private Philanthropy and Public Needs, 20
Committee for Corporate Support of American Universities, 10
Common Cause, 8
Conference Board, 19, 21
Congress, U.S., 6, 16
Conservative Caucus, 9
Consumer Alert, 8, 42
Council on Religion and International Affairs, 14

Dartmouth College, 3
Democracy Project, 41
Democratic party, 7, 33
Depew, Chauncey, 13
Does Big Business Rule America? (Hessen), 28
Drexel Institute, 13
Dryden, John, 29

Economic Recovery Act of 1981, 15
Emory University, 42
Encounter, 42
Ethics and Public Policy Center, 9, 28, 32, 37, 42
Exxon, 8, 21

61

Federal Election Commission, 6-7
Federal Election Reform Act of 1974, 6
Federalist Papers, 6
Filer Commission, 1
First Amendment, 6
First National Bank v. *Bellotti,* 7
FitzGerald, Frances, 2
Ford Foundation, 1-2, 14, 21, 22
Ford, Henry, I, 22
Ford, Henry, II, 1-2, 21
Foundation for Public Affairs, 8, 41-42
Freedom of Information Act, 35
Free to Choose (Friedman), 17
Fremont-Smith, Marion R., 15
Friedman, Milton, 12, 16-17, 27

Galbraith, John Kenneth, 3
General Motors, 21
Gierke, Otto von, 3
Guide to Public Policy Research Organizations (Institute for Educational Affairs), 42

Harriss, C. Lowell, 10-11
Heritage Foundation, 26, 31-32, 35, 38, 42
Holmes, Oliver Wendell, 14
Hoover Institution, 32, 35, 38, 41-42
Hopkins, Johns, 13
House of Representatives, U.S., 35
Hudson Institute, 42

IEA Report, The (Institute for Educational Affairs), 42
Infant Formula Action Coalition (INFACT), 35
Insider Newsletter (Heritage Foundation), 42
Institute for Contemporary Studies, 38, 41-42
Institute for Educational Affairs (IEA), 42
Institute for Policy Studies, 9, 37, 41
Institute for Religion and Democracy, 37
Internal Revenue Act, 15
Internal Revenue Service (IRS), 33, 41

Johns Hopkins University, 13
Joyce, Michael, 41, 43
Julius II, Pope, 29

Kirkpatrick Jeane J., 32, 38
Kristol, Irving, vii, 10, 21-22, 36, 38, 42-43

Larry, Richard, 43
Law and Economics Center, 8, 42

Madison, James, 6-7
Marcus, Philip, 43
Marshall, John, 3
Marxism-Leninism, 25, 37
McLuhan, Marshall, 33
McMichael, Dan, 43
Media Institute, 31
Michelangelo, 29
Mobil Corporation, 5, 21
Moral Majority, 36

Nader, Ralph, 8, 22
National Association of Manufacturers, 6, 41
National Bureau of Economic Research, 42
National Chamber Foundation, 36
National Committee for an Effective Congress, 9
National Information Bureau, 41
National News Council, 9
National Taxpayers Union, 8
New York Times, 32
Niebuhr, Reinhold, 25
North Atlantic Treaty Organization (NATO), 31
Novak, Michael, 10, 12, 38, 43

Oil Muddle, The: Control vs. Competition (Ramsey), 28
Olin Foundation, 41
OPEC (Organization of Petroleum Exporting Countries), 5, 7

Pacific Legal Foundation, 9
Packard, David, 10
Philanthropy and the Business Corporation (Fremont-Smith), 15
Policy Networks (Foundation for Public Affairs), 42
Princeton University, 15
Public Broadcasting Service, 17
Public Interest Economics Center, 8
Public Interest Profiles (Foundation for Public Affairs), 8, 41
Public Research Syndicated, 42

Radio Moscow, 25
Ramsey, James B., 28
Reagan, Ronald, 5, 32, 35, 38
Red Cross, 14-15

INDEX

Republican party, 7, 23
Rochester, Earl of; *see* Wilmot, John
Rochester, University of, 11
Rockefeller Foundation, 14
Rockfeller, John D., 13
Rogers, David, 7

Schlesinger, Arthur, Jr., 38
Senate, U.S., 35
Simon, William E., 10, 42
Sistine Chapel, 29
SmithKline Beckman, vii, 6
Soviet Union, 25, 34
Sowell, Thomas, 38
Stanford, Leland, 13
Stanford Research Institute, 29
Stanford University, 10, 13
Stein, Herbert, 38
Supreme Court, U.S., 7

United Nations, 32
United States, 1-2, 4, 14, 19, 23-25, 35-36, 40

United States Steel, 21
United Technologies, 6
United Way, 7, 22

Wallis, W. Allen, 10-12, 15-16
Wall Street Journal, 32
Washington, D.C., 6, 8-9, 13, 31, 36-38, 41
Washington University Medical School, 13
White House, 37
Wilderness Society, 8
Will, George F., 38
Wilmot, John, 29
Wilson, James Q., 38
Women's Equity Action League, 8
Work in America Institute, 41
World Health Organization, 35
Worldwatch Institute, 41

YMCA, 14

ETHICS AND PUBLIC POLICY REPRINTS

22. **Dictatorships and Double Standards: A Critique of U.S. Policy,** *Jeane Kirkpatrick*
A carefully documented indictment of the Carter administration's selective indignation toward allied and friendly Third World regimes.

24. **Crusade Against the Corporation: Church Militants on the March,** *Herman Nickel*
Church activists, working through the Interfaith Center on Corporate Responsibility, are leading a campaign to curb the power of multinational corporations. A major objective is to control the sale of infant formula in the Third World; their major tactic is to boycott Nestlé products.

25. **America the Enemy: Profile of a Revolutionary Think Tank,** *Rael Jean Isaac*
A thorough examination of the Institute for Policy Studies suggests that it is the hub of a revolutionary political network masquerading as an authentic "think tank."

29. **Solzhenitsyn and American Democracy,** *George F. Will and Michael Novak*
Two respected political commentators admire Solzhenitsyn's insistence that an enduring society must have deep spiritual roots but find he expects too much from democracy.

31. **Sanctifying Revolution: Mainline Churchmen Turn Radical**
Rael Jean Isaac and Erich Isaac
In pursuing justice and "liberation," mainline church leaders have increasingly supported revolutionary, sometimes even violent, means.

32. **Education, Character, and American Schools,** *Gerald Grant*
Students must once again be taught to respect a common code of behavior even if it is a "provisional morality" that they may later revise.

33. **The New Defenders of Capitalism,** *Norman Podhoretz*
The traditional hostility of intellectuals toward market enterprise shows signs of reversal; many now argue that capitalism is the most productive system and increases freedom of choice.

34. **Moral Implications of Energy**
William G. Pollard, Frederick S. Carney, and Thomas J. Reese, S.J.
A nuclear physicist (and Episcopal priest), a professor of Christian ethics, and an editor of *America* reflect on the moral and theological implications of nuclear energy.

35. **How to Lose a War: The Press and Viet Nam,** *Robert Elegant*
A veteran Asia correspondent says the Viet Nam war was lost not on the battlefield but in the minds of Western liberals whose views dominated the prestige press in the United States.

36. **Why Latin America Is Poor,** *Michael Novak*
Latin American poverty is caused not by North American wealth or multinational corporations but by domestic social and cultural forces rooted in the political and economic institutions and world view of the Spanish conquerors.

37. **On the Brink: The Myth of German Anti-Americanism,** *Uwe Siemon-Netto*
The German left wing's "long march" through the courts, schools, churches, media, and other institutions has had considerable success, but the great majority of the German people do not support the radical demand for the withdrawal of U.S. troops.

38. **The Media Elite and American Values,** *S. Robert Lichter and Stanley Rothman*
From interviews with 240 journalists and broadcasters the authors conclude that the views of the media elite on major social, economic, and political questions are substantially to the left of those of middle America.

39. **Risk and Nuclear Power: Scientists, Journalists, and the Public**
S. Robert Lichter and Stanley Rothman
A careful survey of nuclear specialists and other scientists shows that those who know most about nuclear power are its strongest supporters.

40. **Nuclear Weapons and the Peace Movement,** *Henry A. Kissinger*
Combining a firm grasp of political realities with the wisdom of experience, the former secretary of state examines all major facets of the nuclear arms debate.

41. **Private Virtues, Public Vices,** *Jeane Kirkpatrick*
The U.S. representative to the United Nations distinguishes between private and public morality and argues that compromise and consensus-building are essential and desirable in the American political system.

**Reprints are $1 each. Postpaid if payment accompanies order.
Orders of $20 or more, 10 per cent discount.**